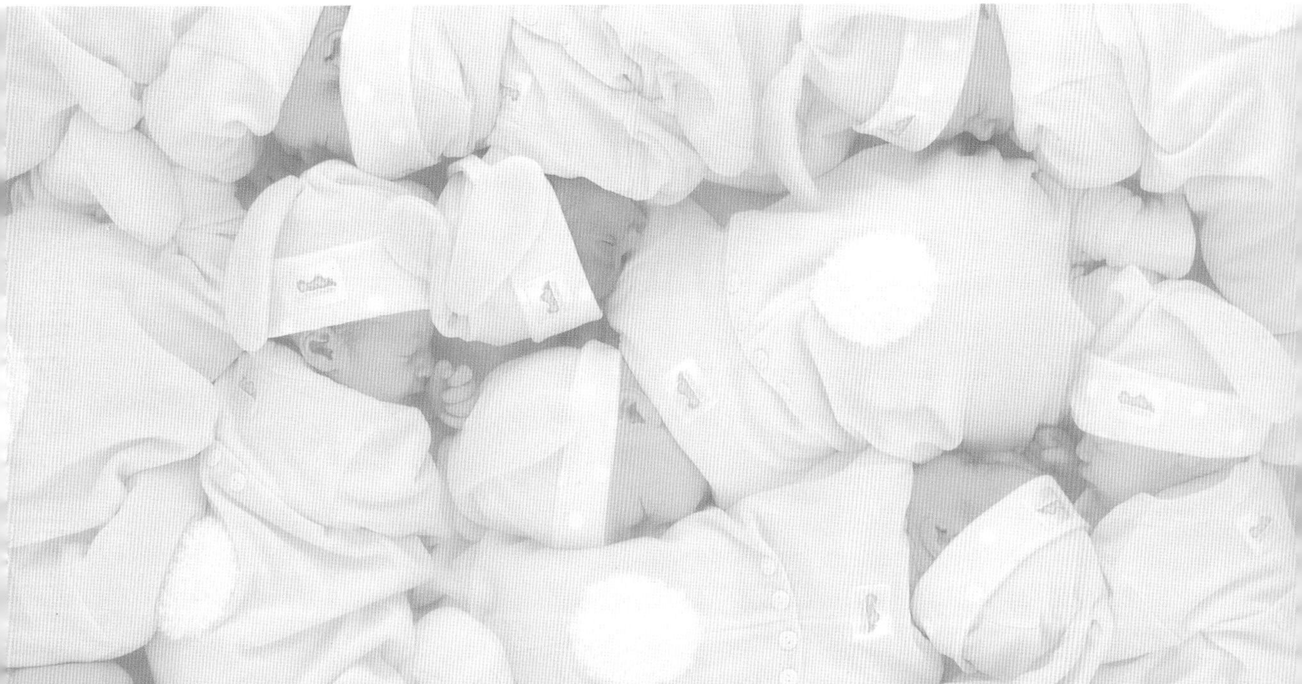

Anne Geddes

My First Five Years

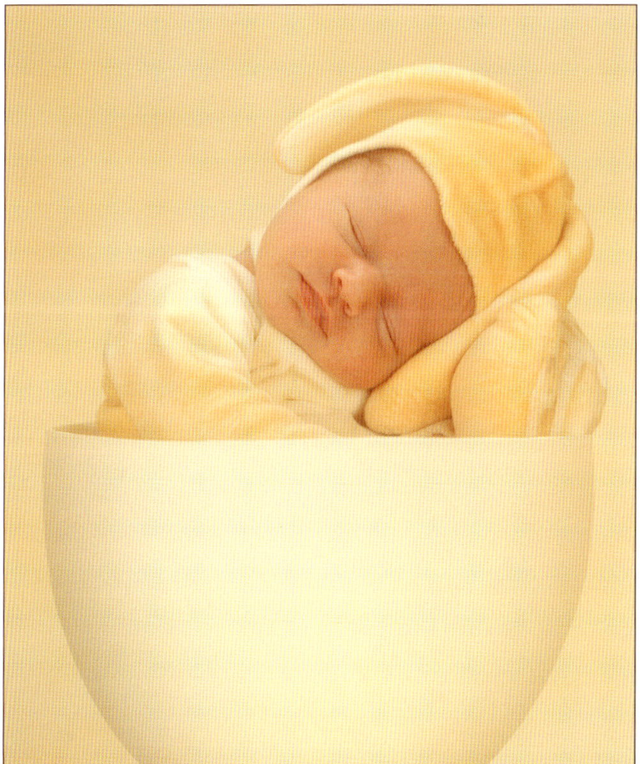

A RECORD OF EARLY CHILDHOOD

CONTENTS

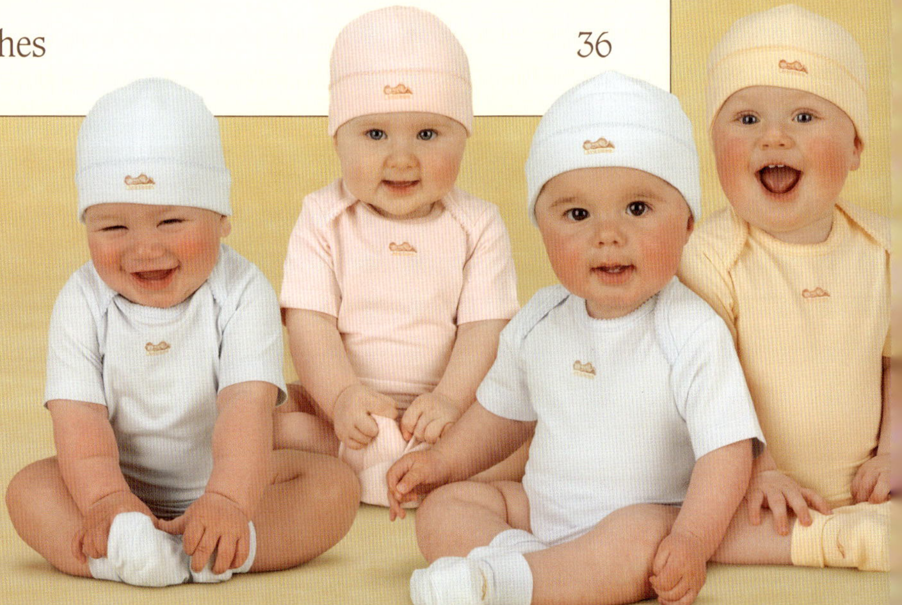

CONTENTS

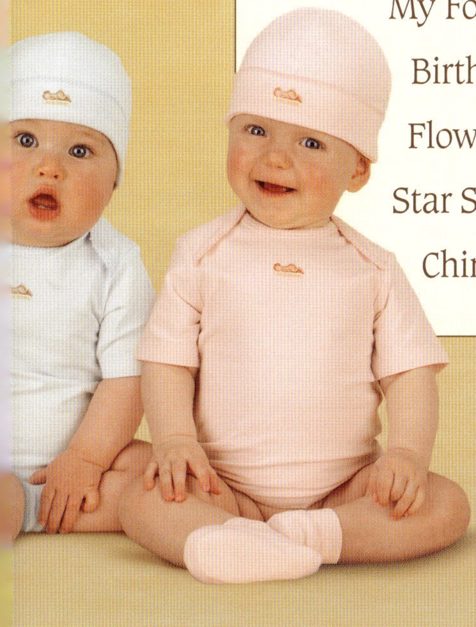

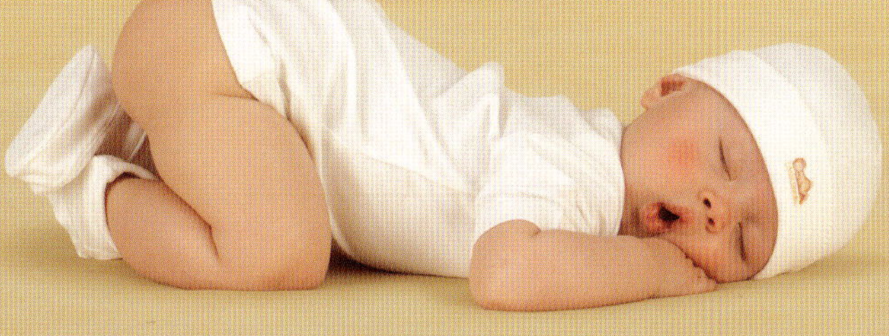

MY BIRTH

My name is ______________________________

____

I was born on ______________________________

at ______________________________

____

The time was ______________________________

I was delivered by ______________________________

I weighed ______________________________

and measured ______________________________

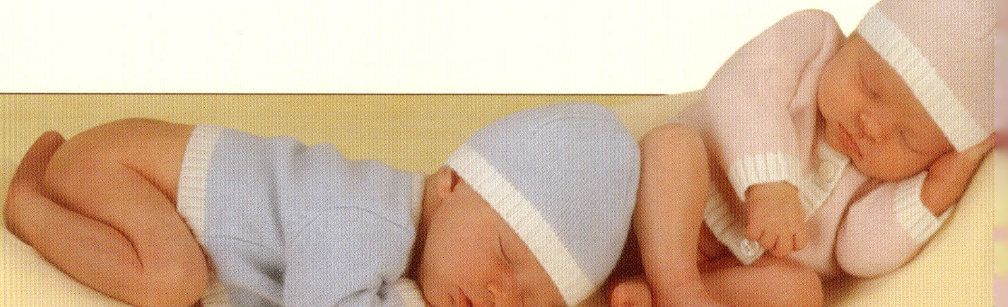

My eyes were ______

______

My hair was ______

______

My skin was ______

______

My belly button was ______

______

______

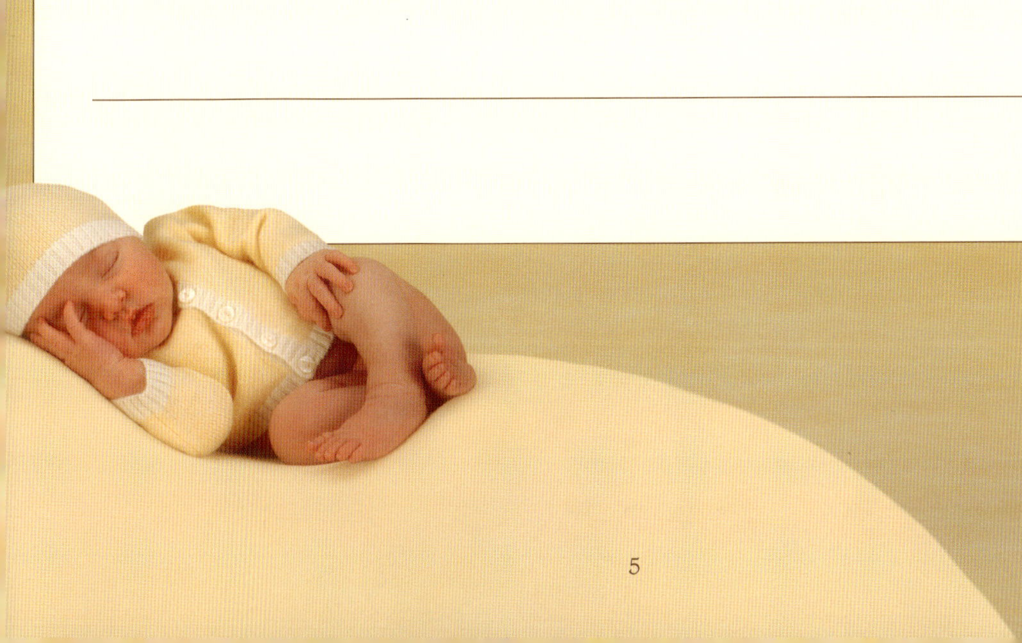

MEMENTOS

My Birth Announcement

A lock of hair

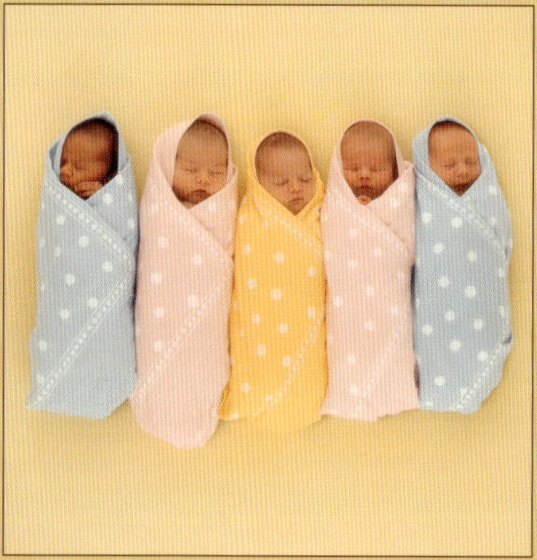

My hospital tag

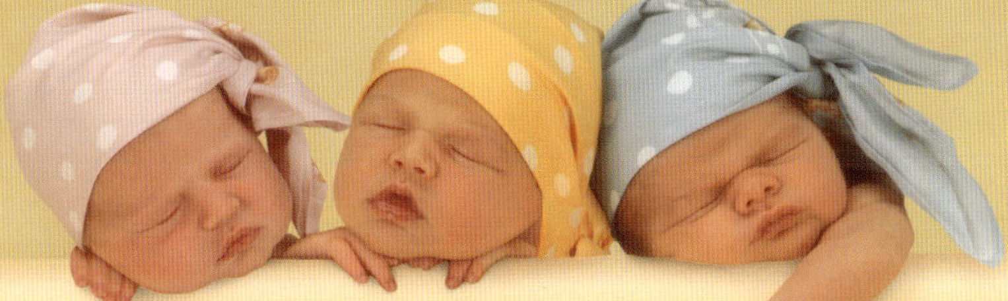

NEWSPAPER CLIPPINGS

What was happening in the world

PHOTOGRAPHS

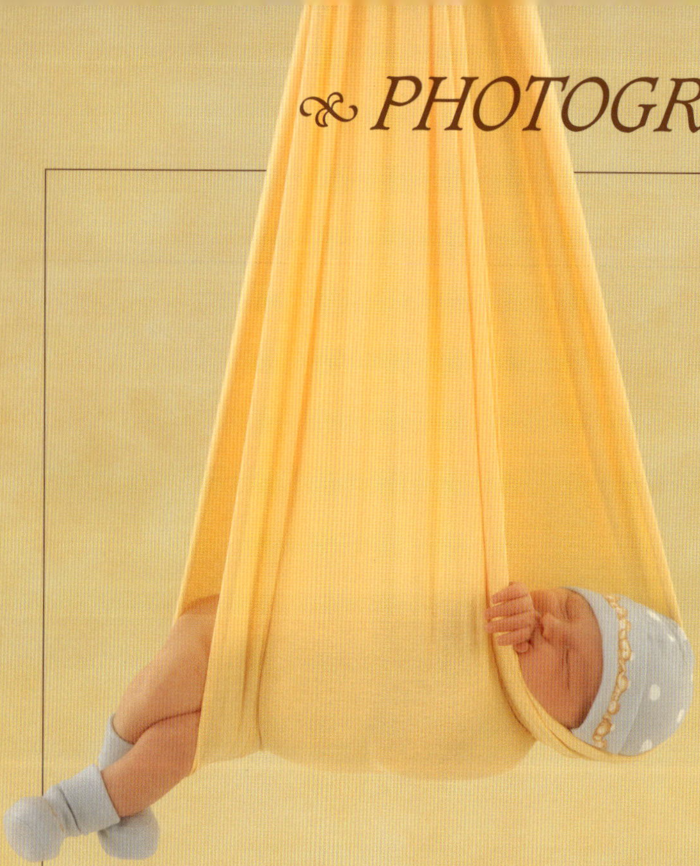

PHOTOGRAPHS

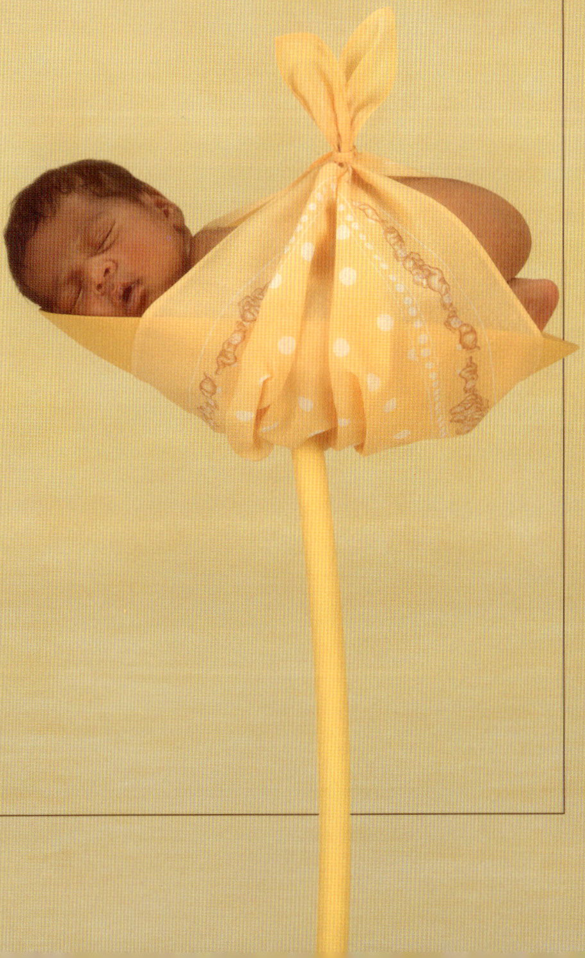

SPECIAL MESSAGES

Mother

Father

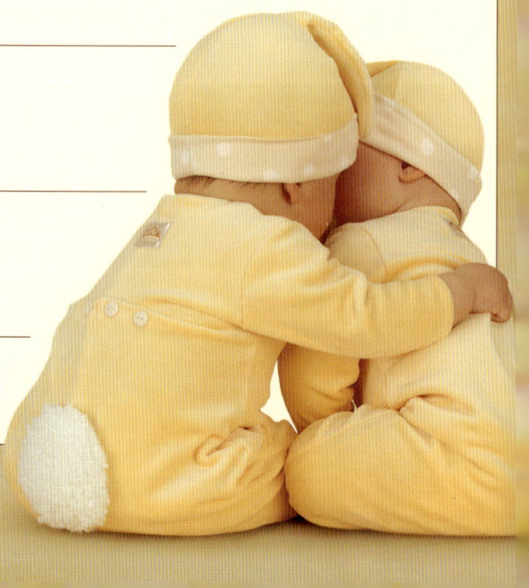

Family

Friends

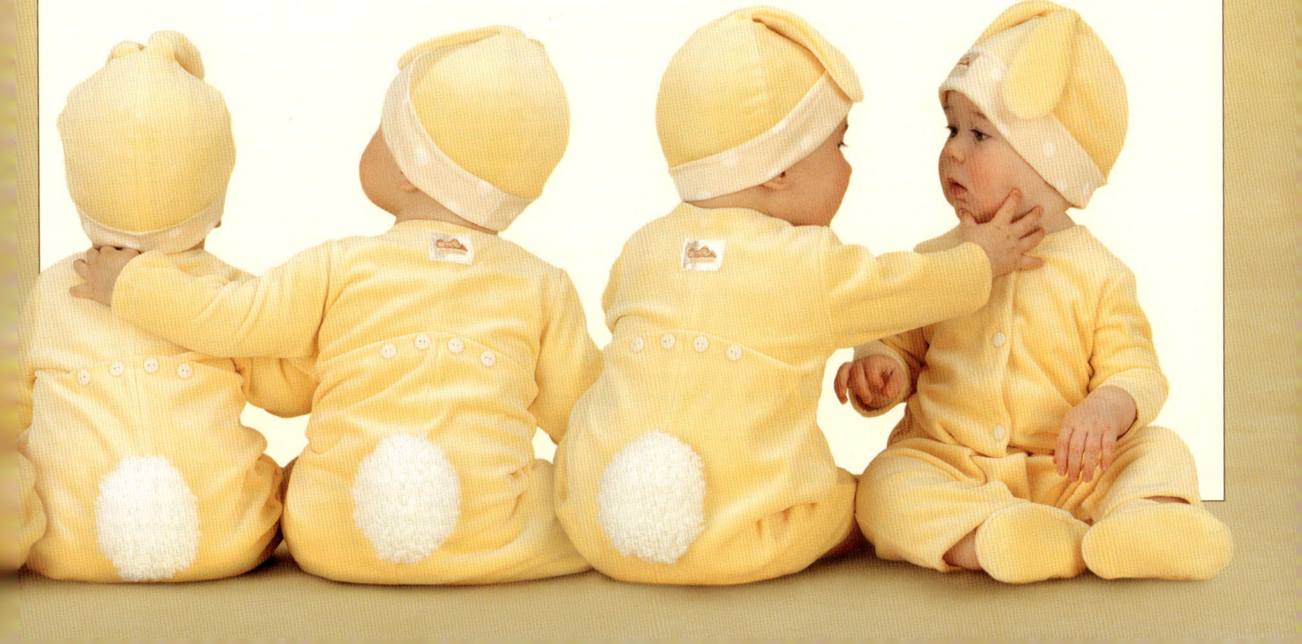

VISITORS & GIFTS

From	*I received*

SIGNS

Star Sign

Chinese Year

Birth Stone

Birth Flower

Birthday Horoscope

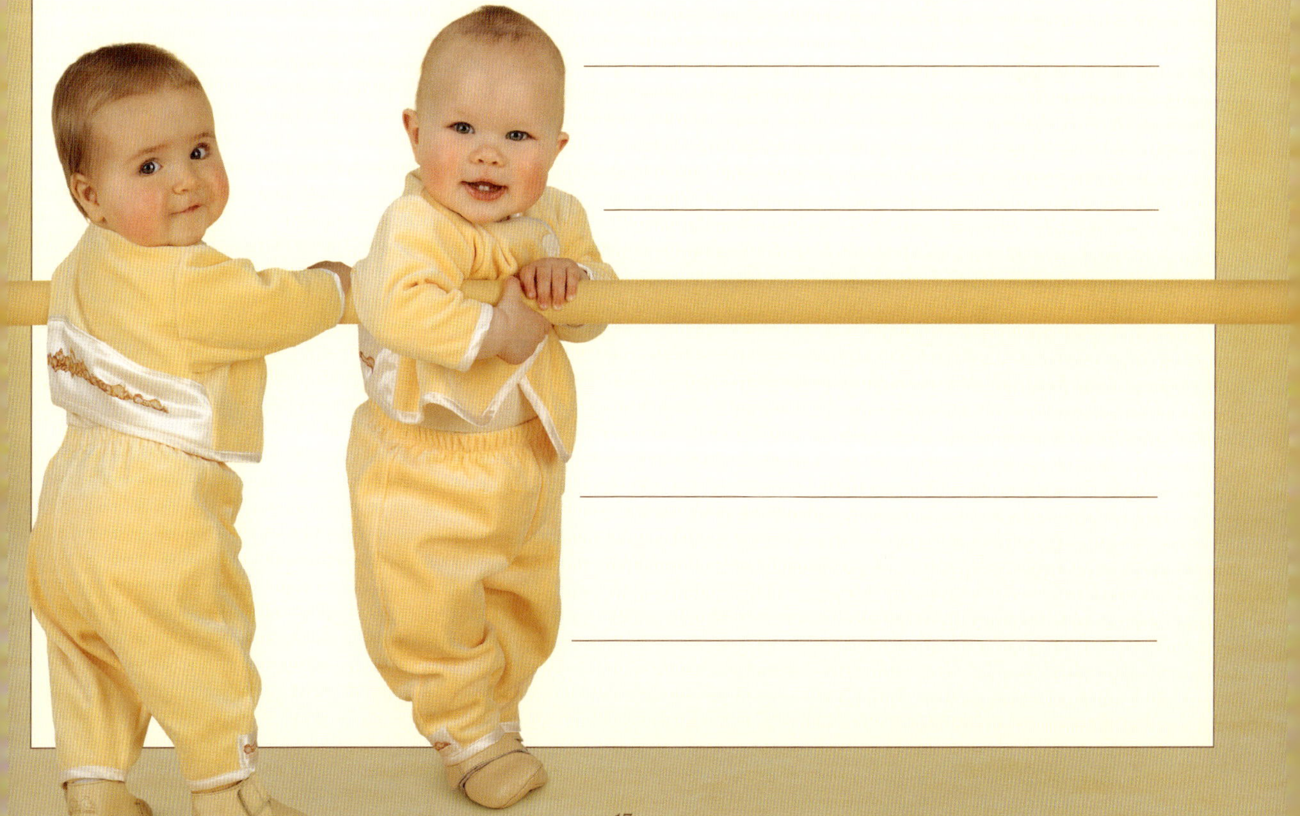

NAMING

My full name is ______________________

My name was chosen by ______________________

because ______________________

My pet names are ______________________

____

Ceremonies celebrating my birth ______________________

____

at ______________________

Comments ______________________

____

____

PHOTOGRAPHS

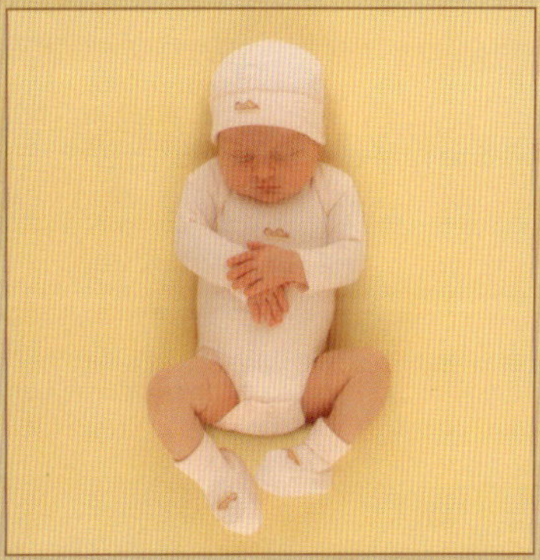
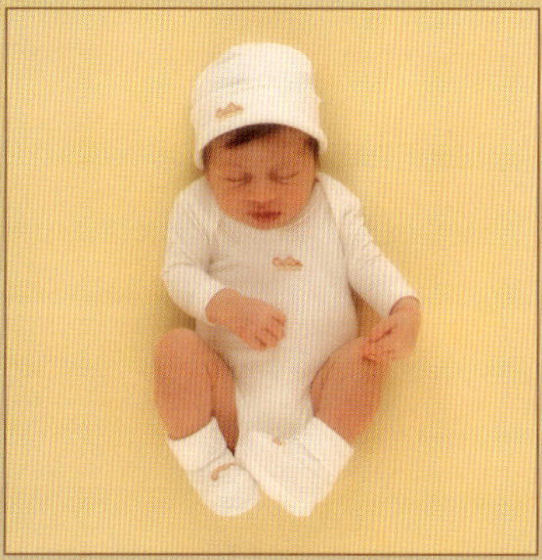
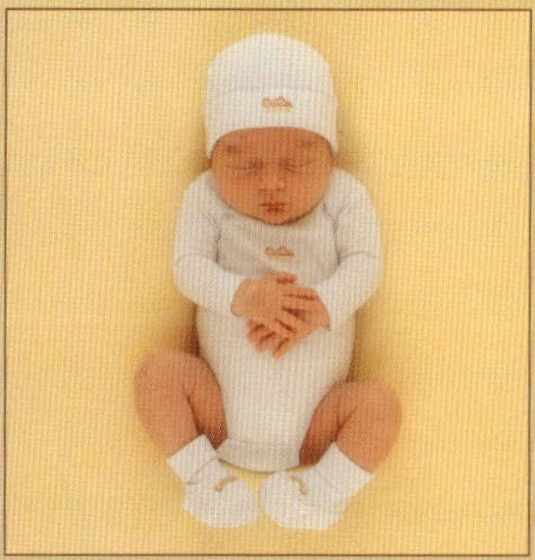

MY FAMILY TREE

Grandfather

Grandfather

Grandmother

Grandmother

Father

Mother

Me

Brothers and Sisters

ATTRIBUTES

My hair is like ______________________________

My skin is like ______________________________

My nose is like ______________________________

My eyes are like ______________________________

My mouth is like ______________________________

My chin is like ______________________________

My cheeks are like ______________________________

Other attributes ______________________________

____

____

____

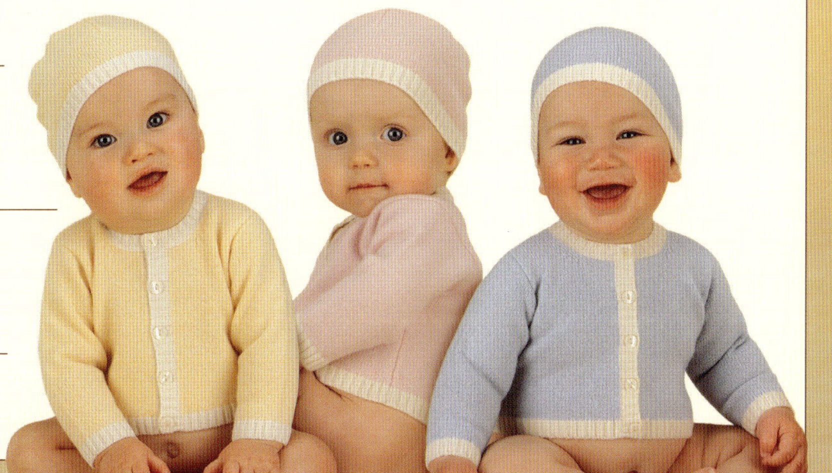

PHOTOGRAPHS

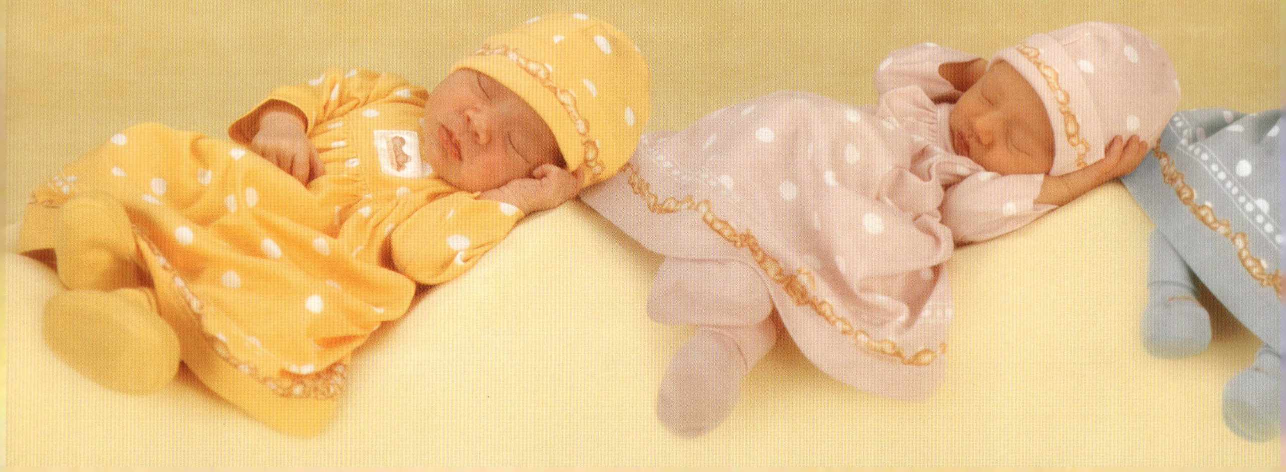

THREE MONTHS

Weight ______________________________

Length ______________________________

Comments ______________________________

____

____

____

____

____

____

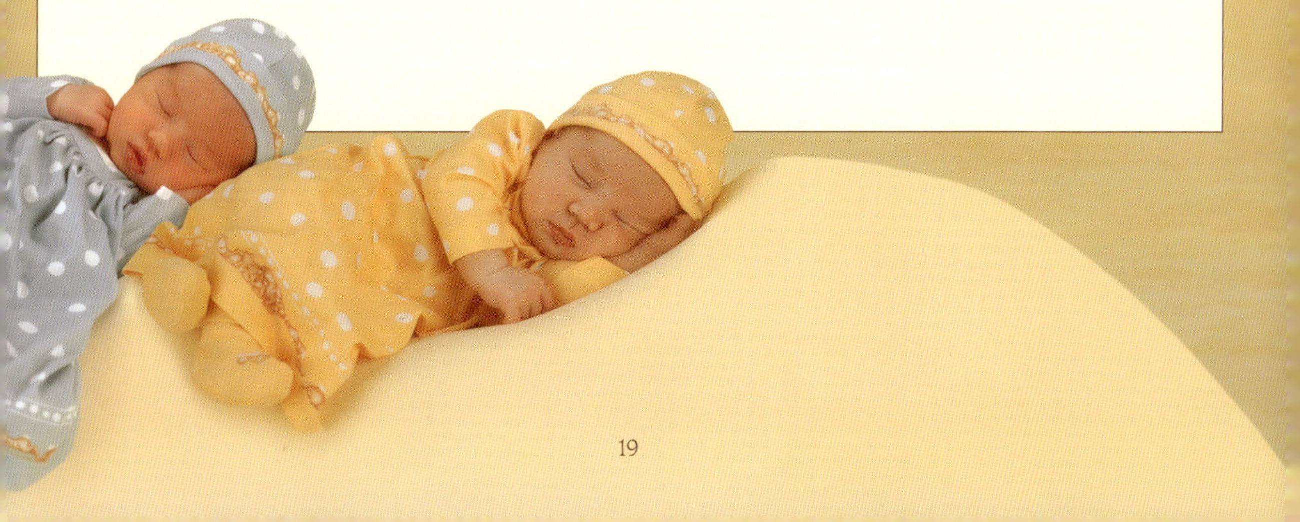

SIX MONTHS

Weight ______________________________

Length ______________________________

Comments ______________________________

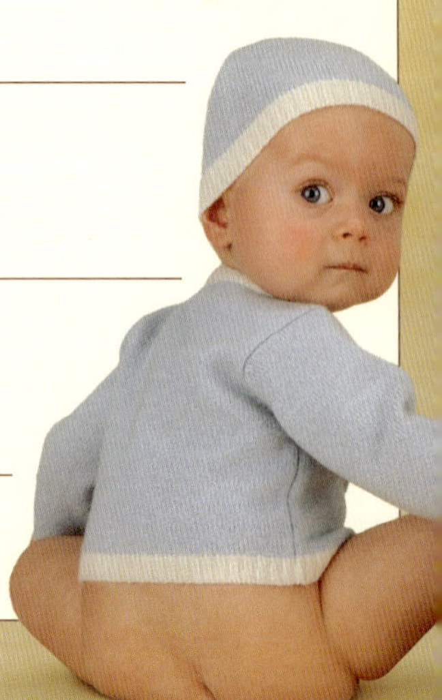

PHOTOGRAPHS

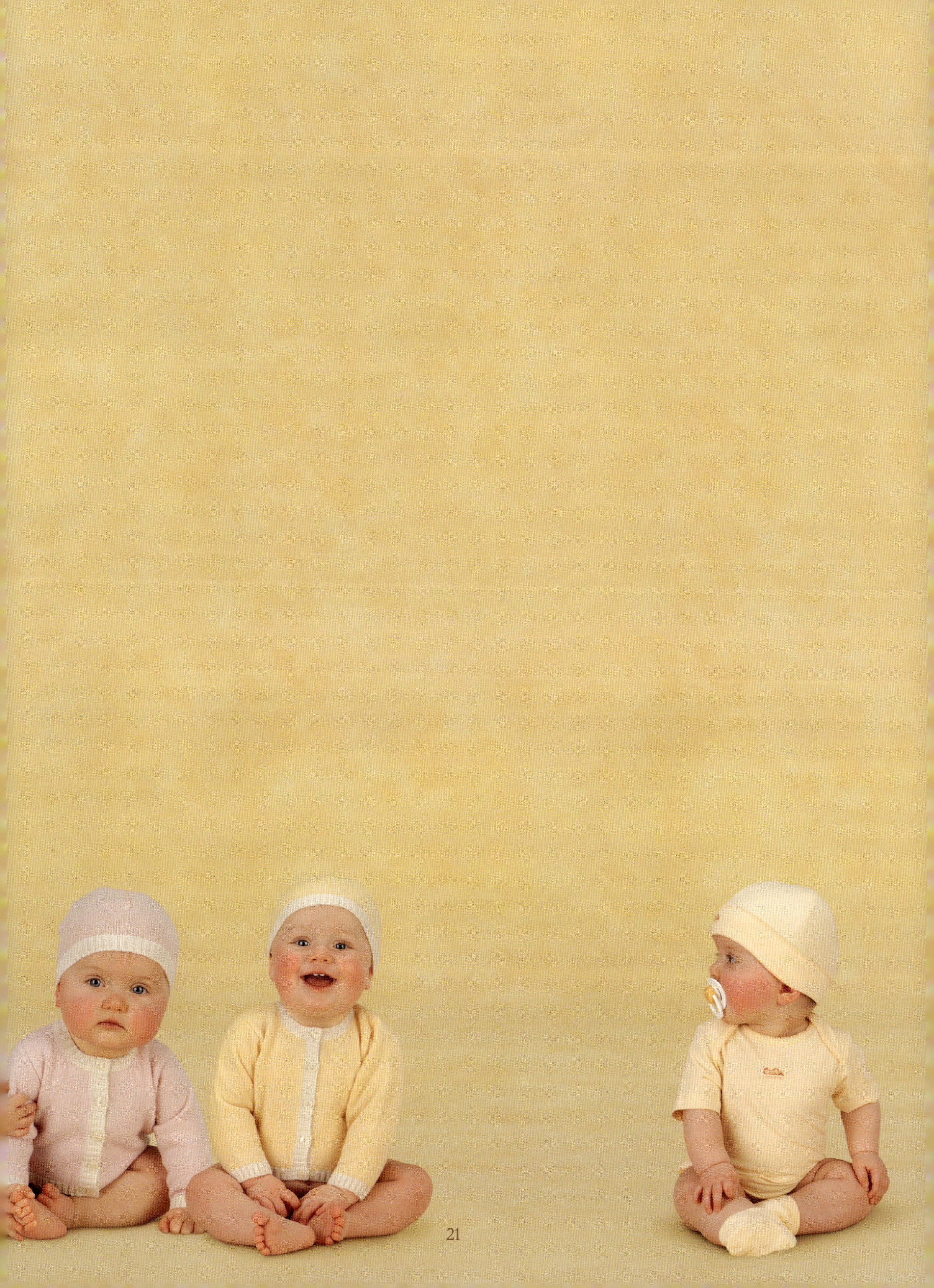

PHOTOGRAPHS

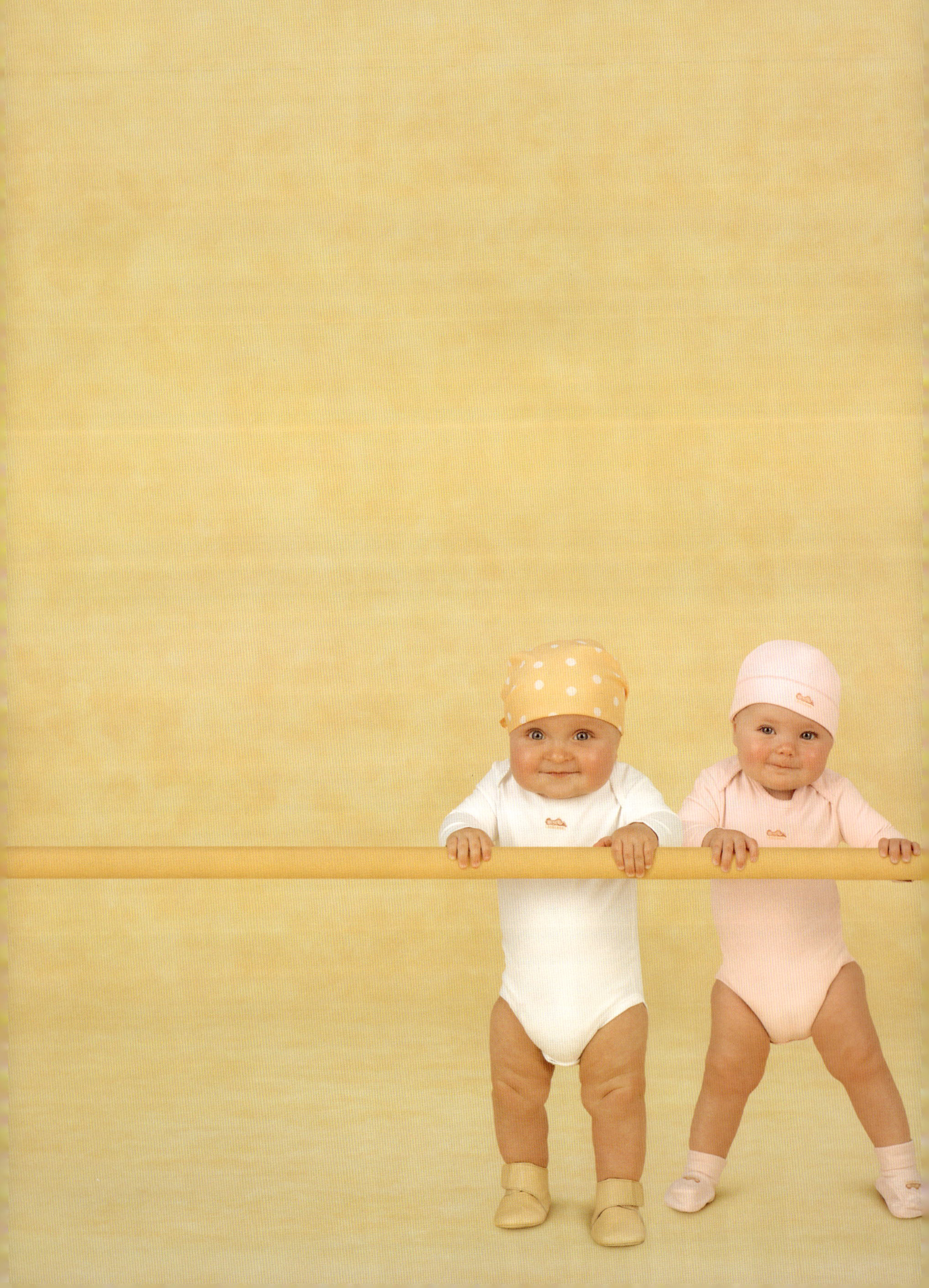

NINE MONTHS

Weight

Length

Comments

MY FIRST BIRDAY

I live at ______________________

My height is ______________________

My weight is ______________________

Sayings ______________________

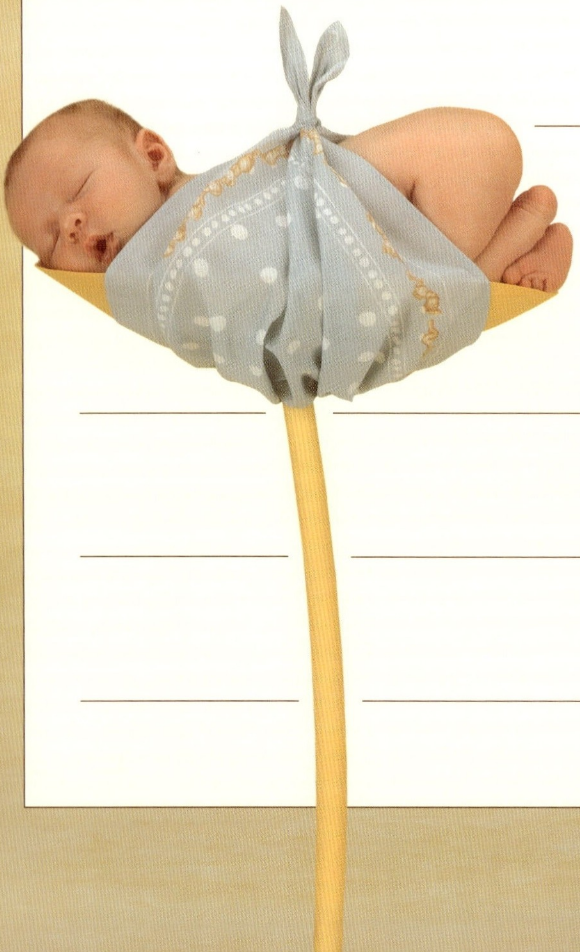

MY PARTY

Date ___

Place ___

Friends & relatives there ___

___

Presents ___

___

___

___

___

___

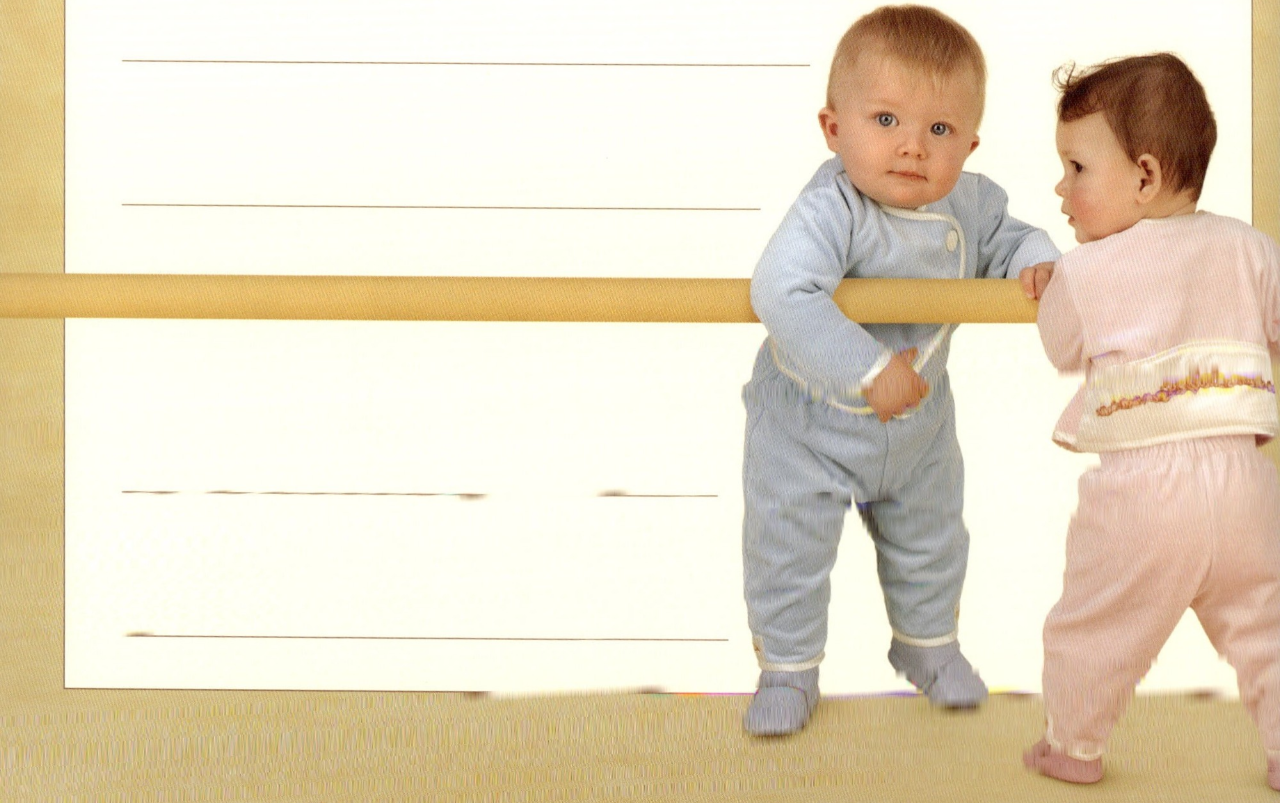

PHOTOGRAPHS

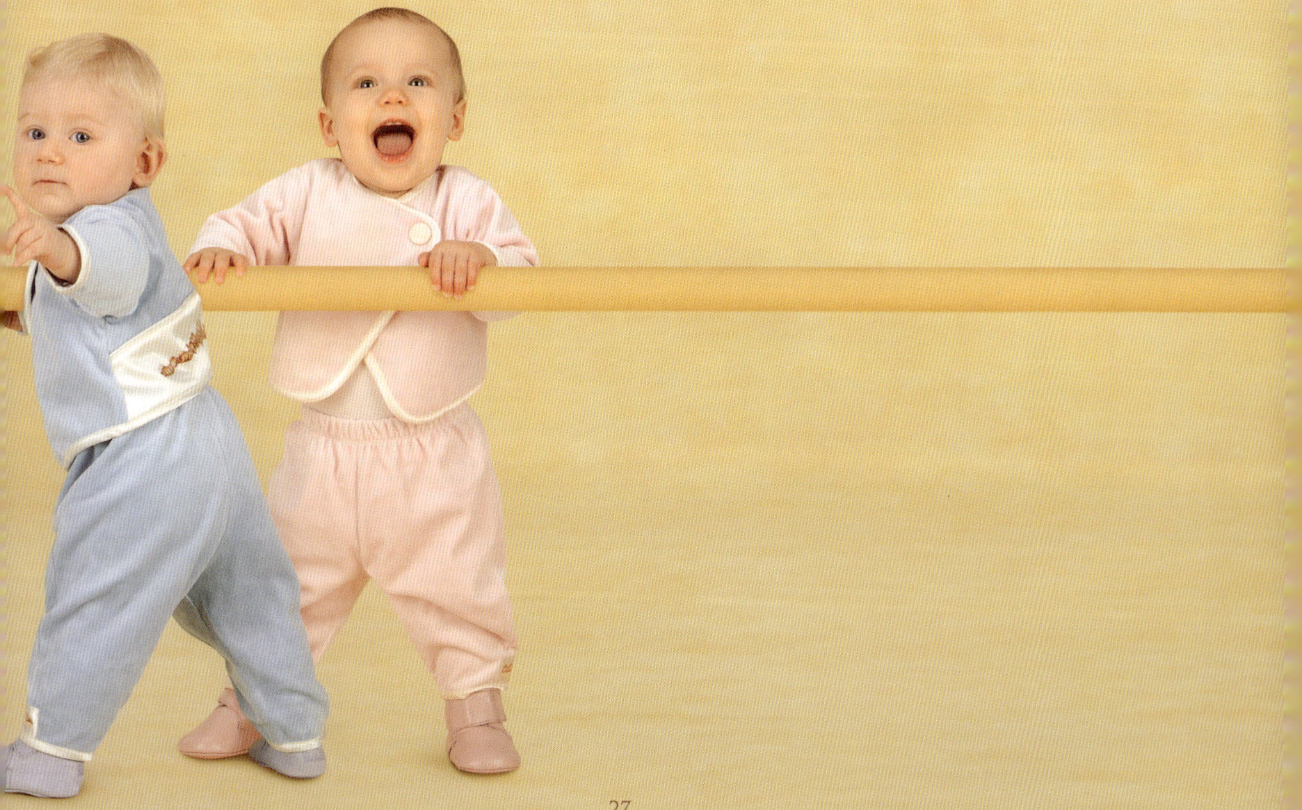

MILESTONES

I first smiled ____________________

I first laughed ____________________

I first grasped a toy ____________________

I first slept through the night ____________________

I first held my head up ____________________

I first rolled over ____________________

I first sat up ____________________

Other milestones ____________________

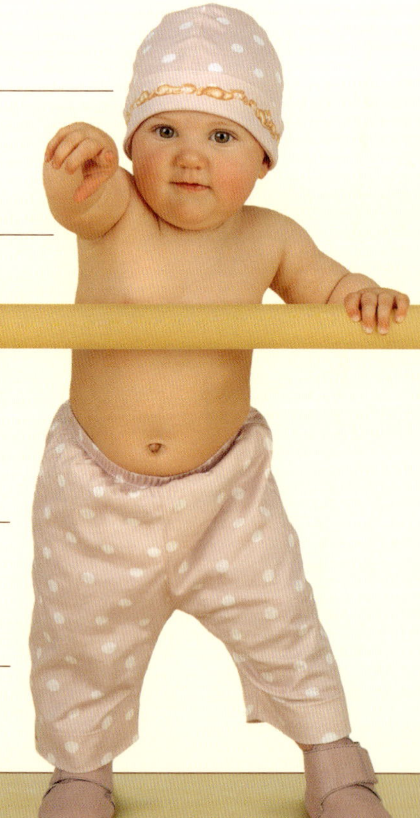

____

____

I first crawled ______________________________

I first stood up ______________________________

I first walked ______________________________

My first tooth ______________________________

My first word ______________________________

Other milestones ______________________________

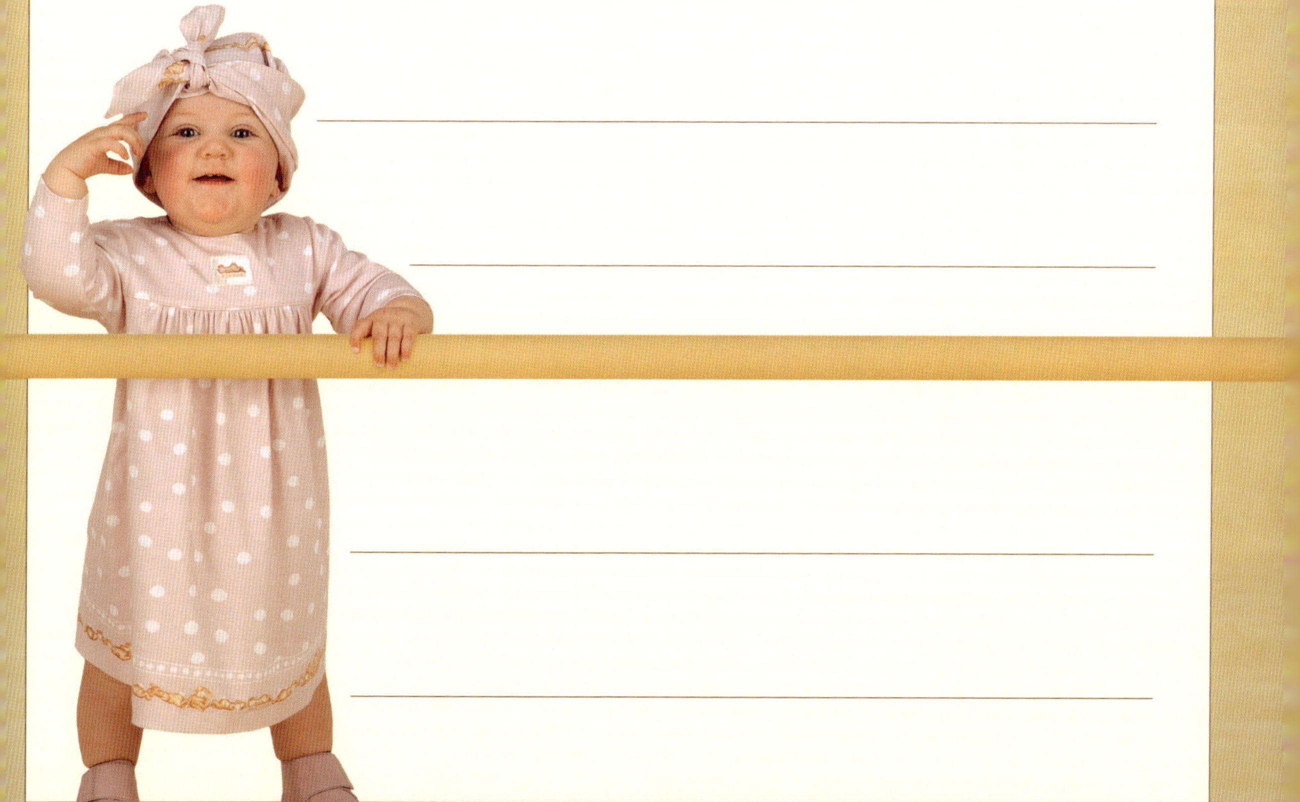

FOOD

My first solid food ______________________

____

I was weaned ______________________

I drank from a cup ______________________

Favorite finger food ______________________

I fed myself ______________________

____

____

____

____

____

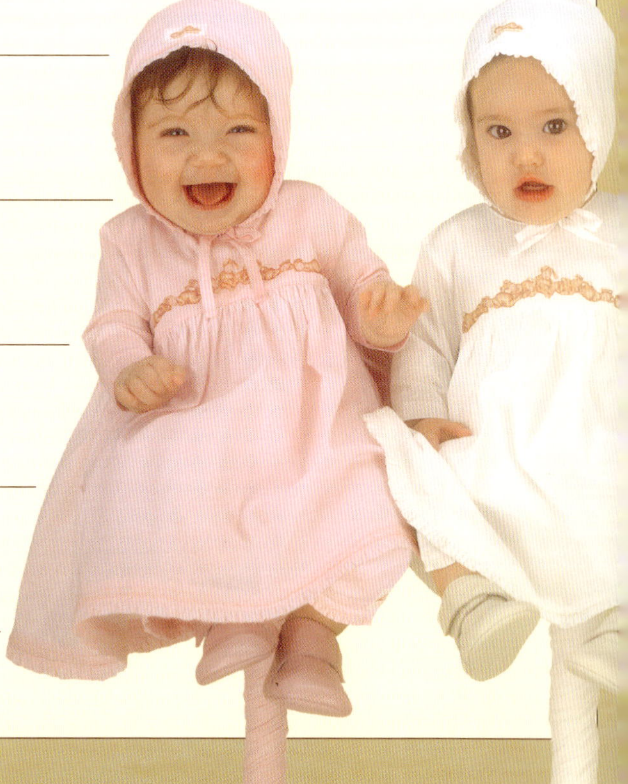

I like ______

I don't like ______

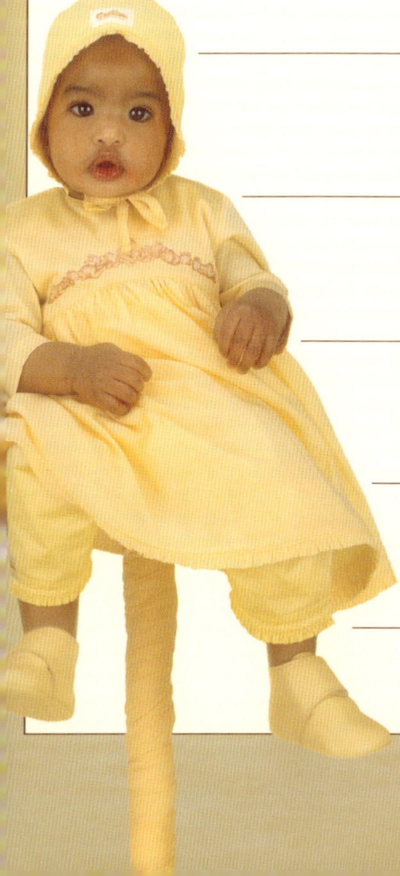

MY FIRST CHRISTMAS

Was at ______________________________

____

Other people there ______________________________

____

____

My presents ______________________________

____

____

____

____

____

PHOTOGRAPHS

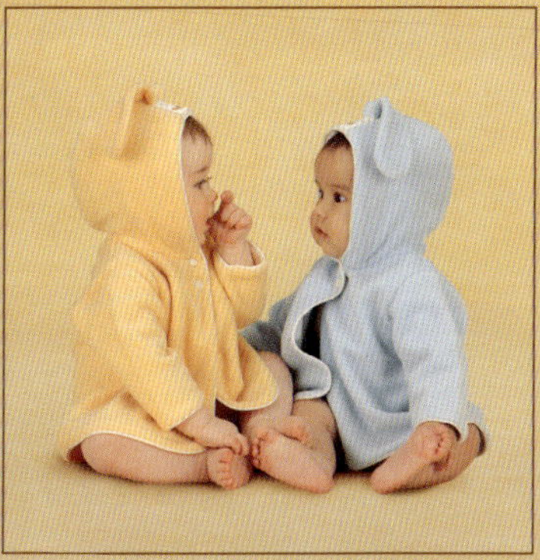 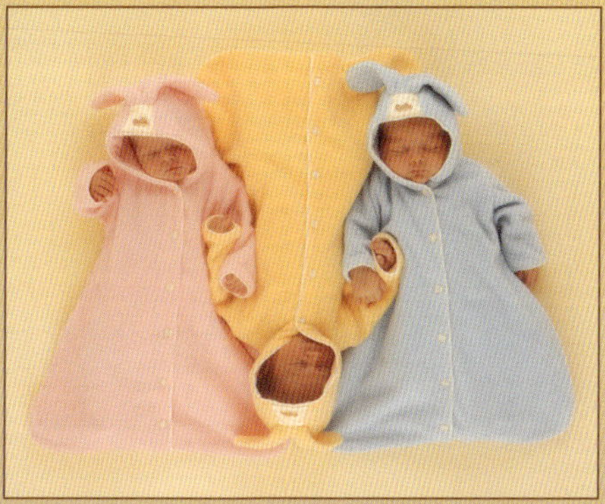 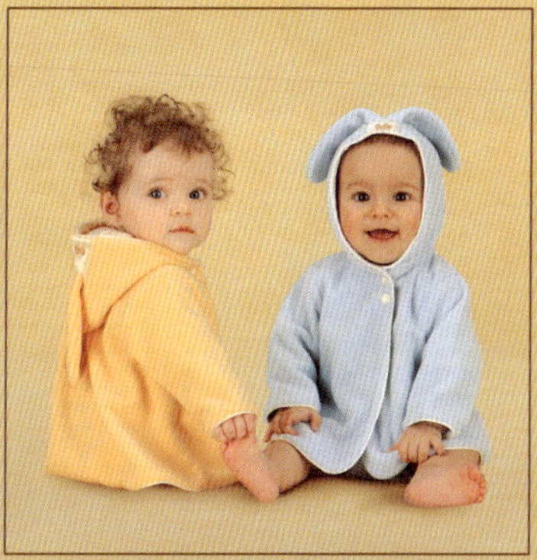

PHOTOGRAPHS

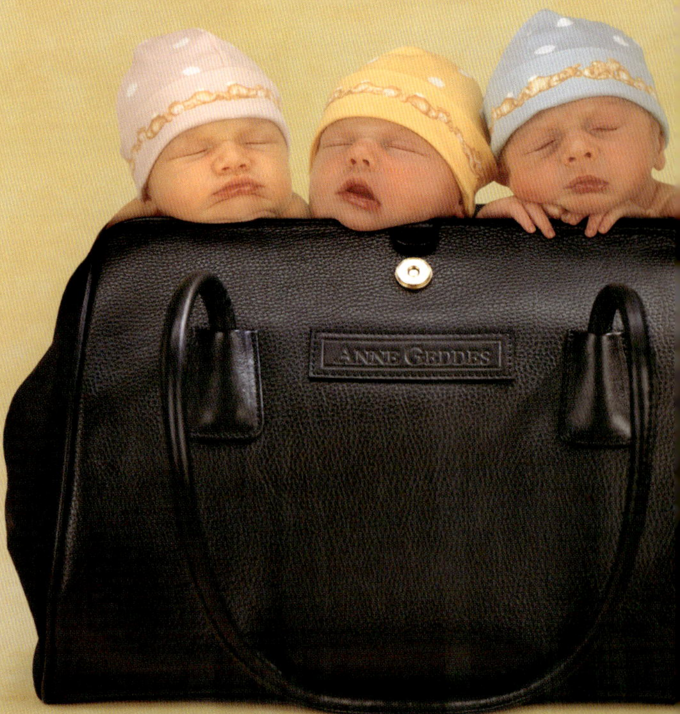

MY FIRST VACATION

Was to ______________________________

Date ______________________________

The weather was ______________________________

Other people there ______________________________

____

____

Comments ______________________________

____

____

____

____

CLOTHES

The first time I dressed myself ______

I wore ______

______

My favorite dress-ups ______

______

I won't wear ______

______

Comments ______

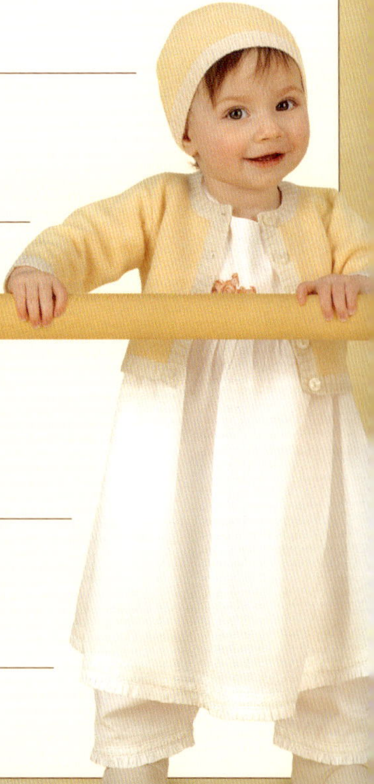

______

______

PHOTOGRAPHS

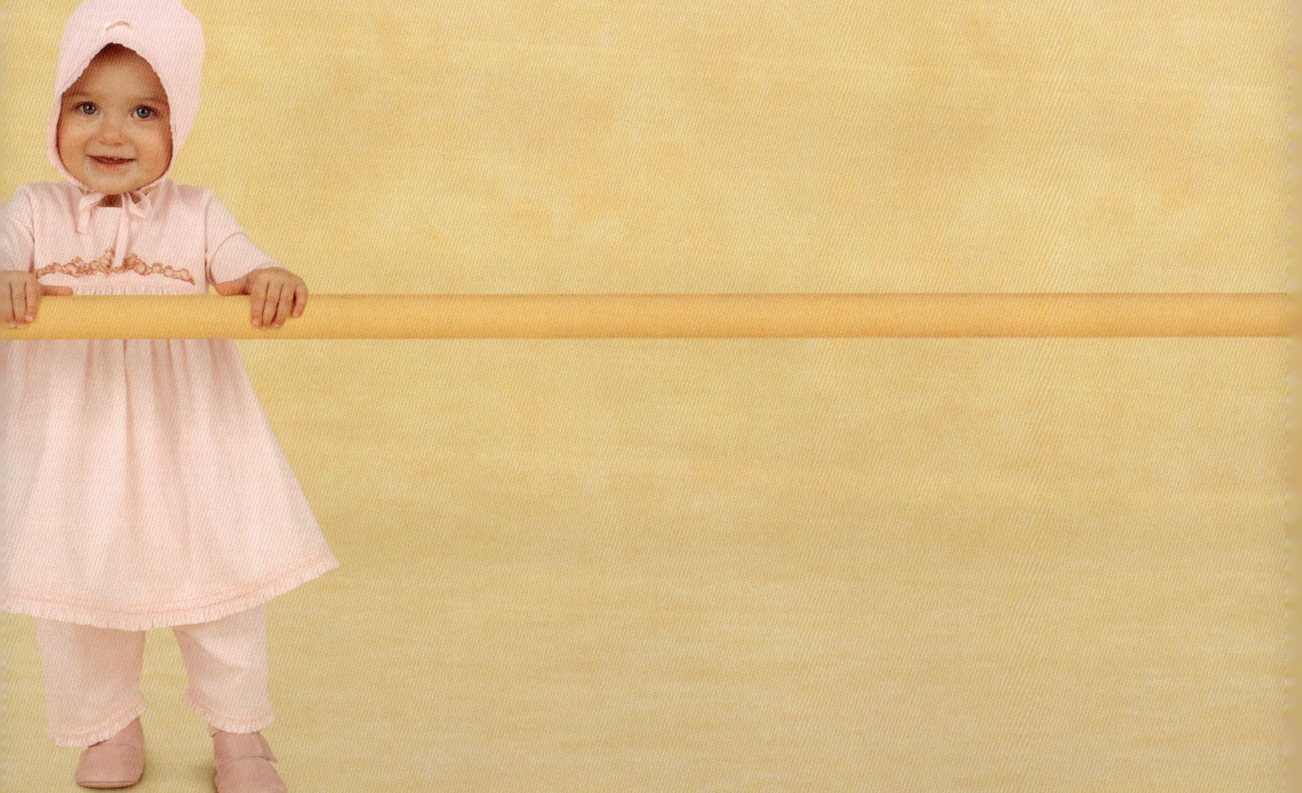

FAVORITES

Music

Rhymes

Clothes

Animals

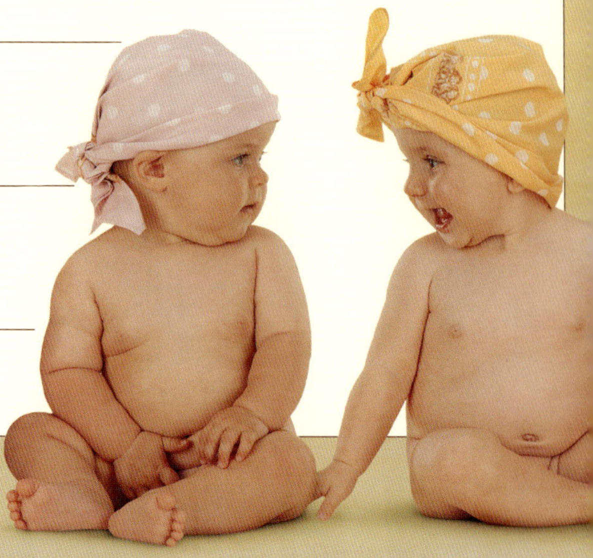

Activities

Television programs

I really don't like

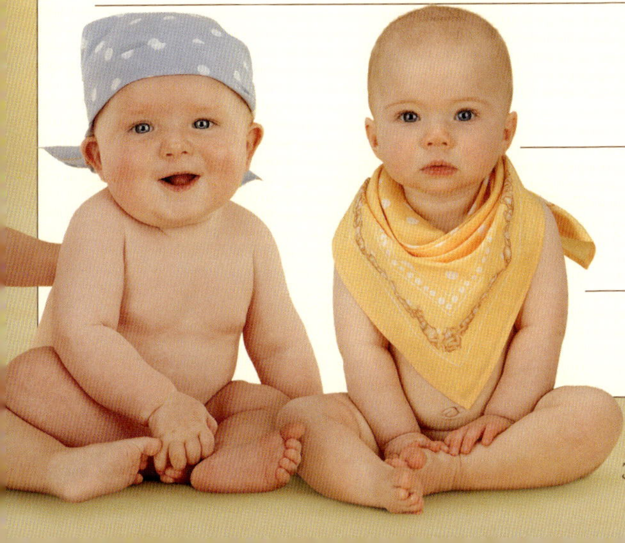

Comments

One Year

Two Years

Three Years

Four Years

Five Years

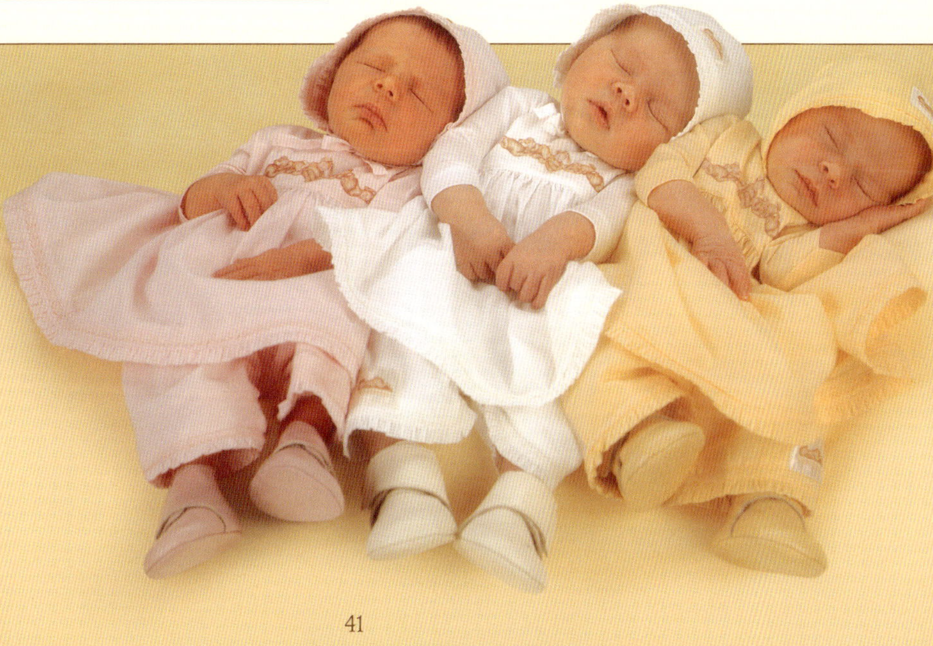

MY SECOND BIRTHDAY

I live at ______________________

My height is ______________________

My weight is ______________________

Sayings ______________________

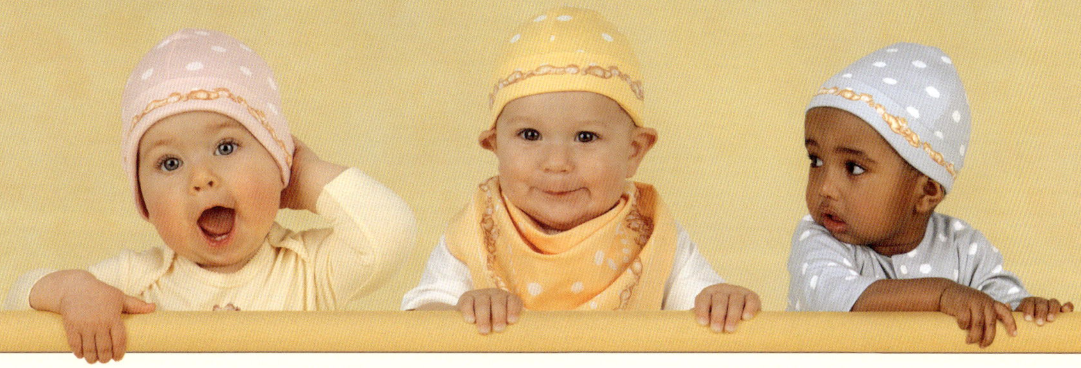

Toys

Pets

Books

MY PARTY

Date ______________________________

Place ______________________________

Friends & relatives there ______________________________

____

Presents ______________________________

____

____

____

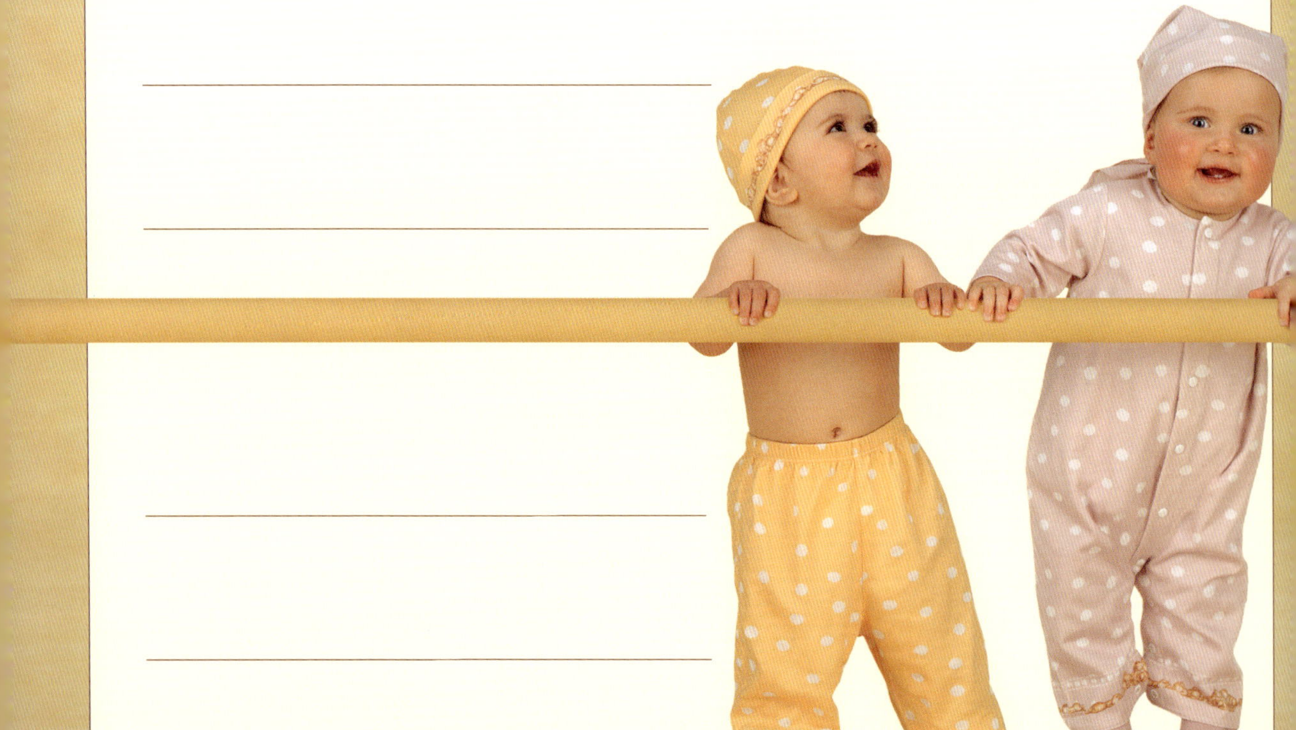

____

____

PHOTOGRAPHS

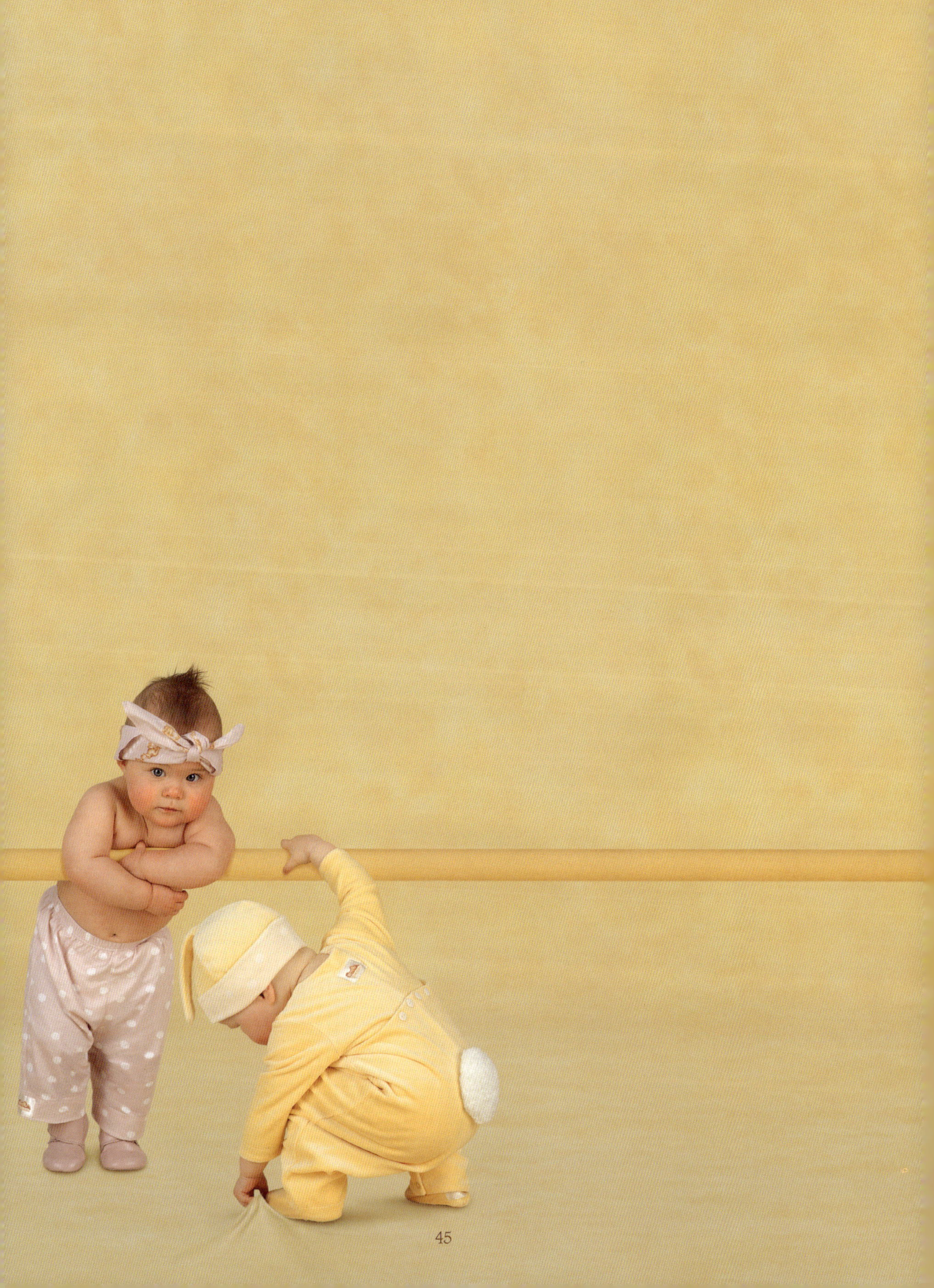

MY THIRD BIRTHDAY

I live at ______________________

My height is ______________________

My weight is ______________________

Sayings ______________________

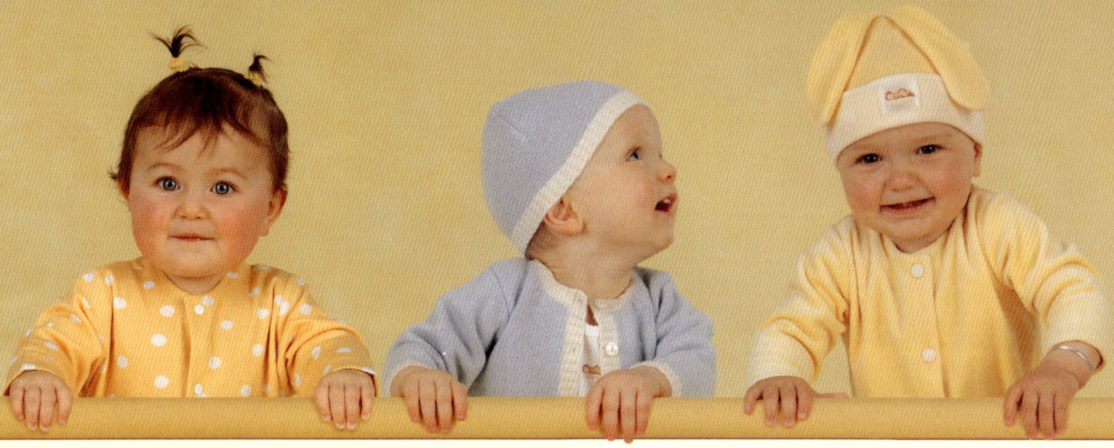

Toys

Pets

Books

PHOTOGRAPHS

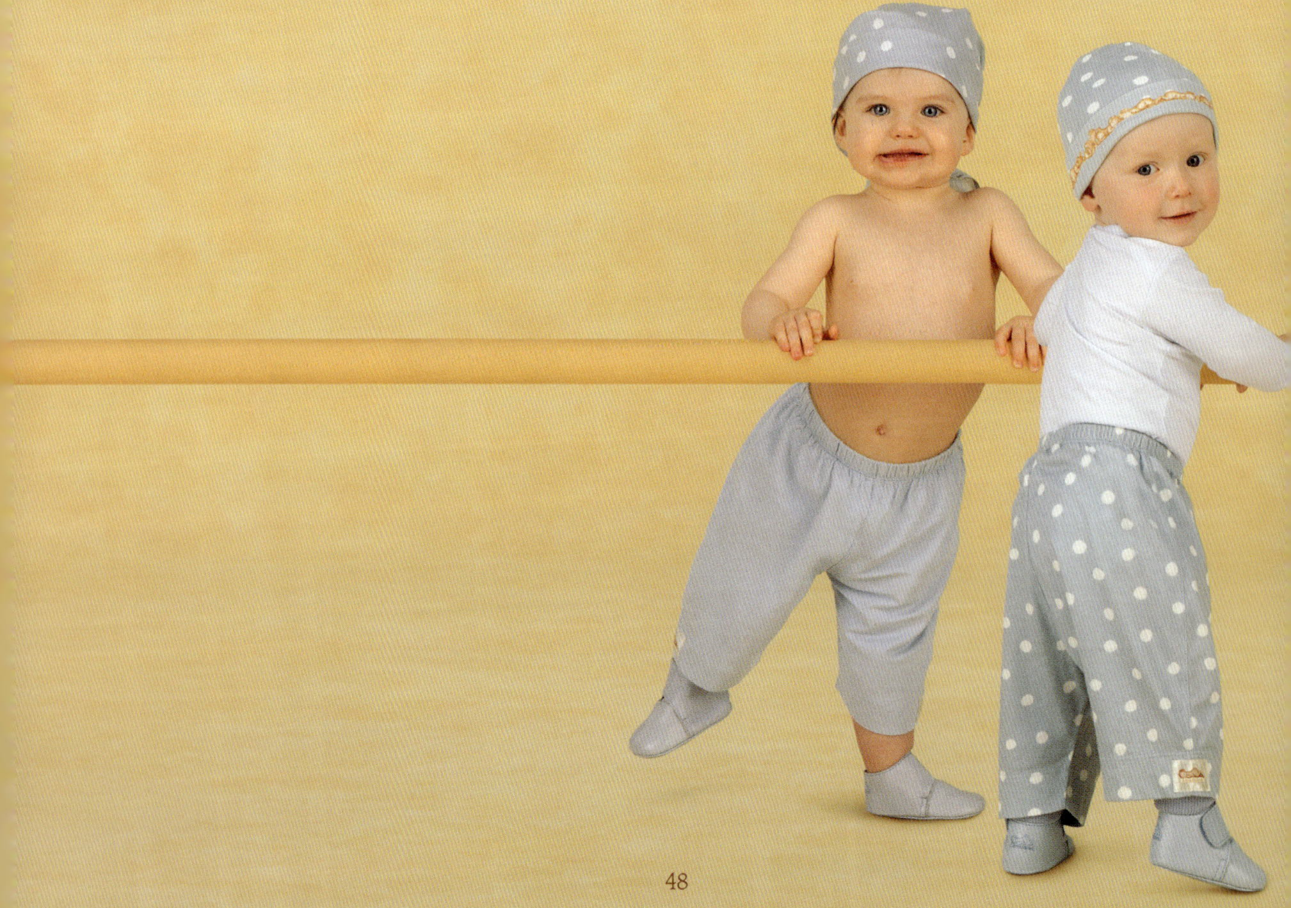

≈ MY PARTY ≈

Date ______________________________

Place ______________________________

Friends & relatives there ______________________________

____

Presents ______________________________

____

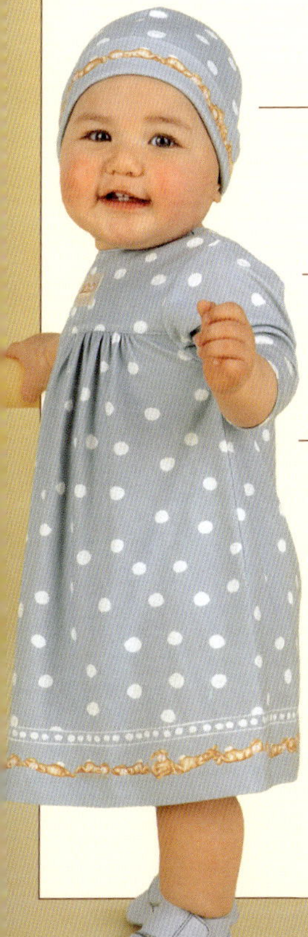

____

____

____

____

____

MY FOURTH BIRTHDAY

I live at ____

My height is ____________________________________

My weight is ____________________________________

Sayings ____

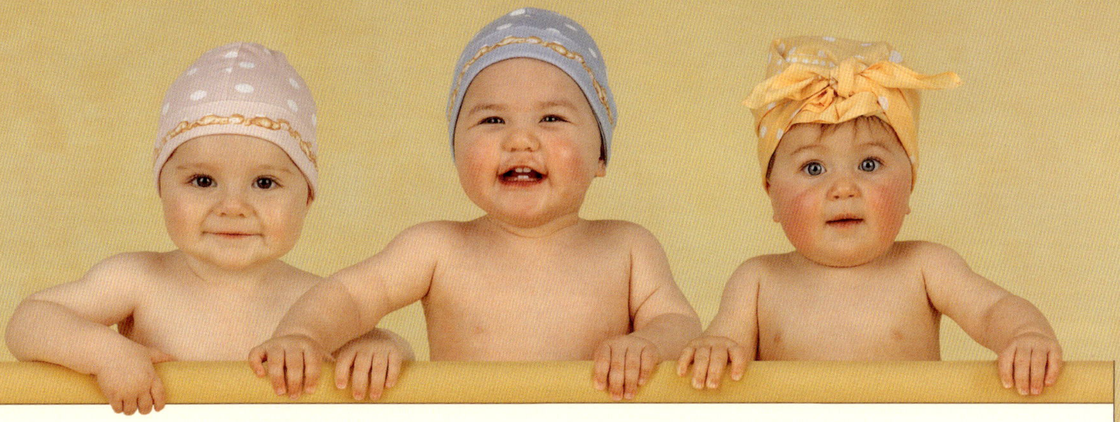

Toys

Pets

Books

MY PARTY

Date ______________________________

Place ______________________________

Friends & relatives there ______________________________

____

Presents ______________________________

____

____

____

____

____

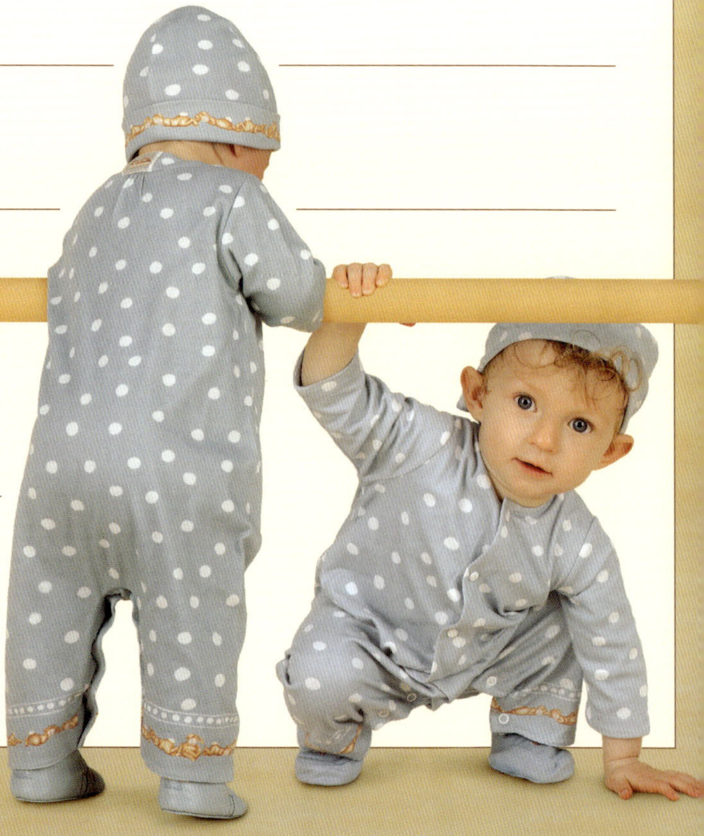

PHOTOGRAPHS

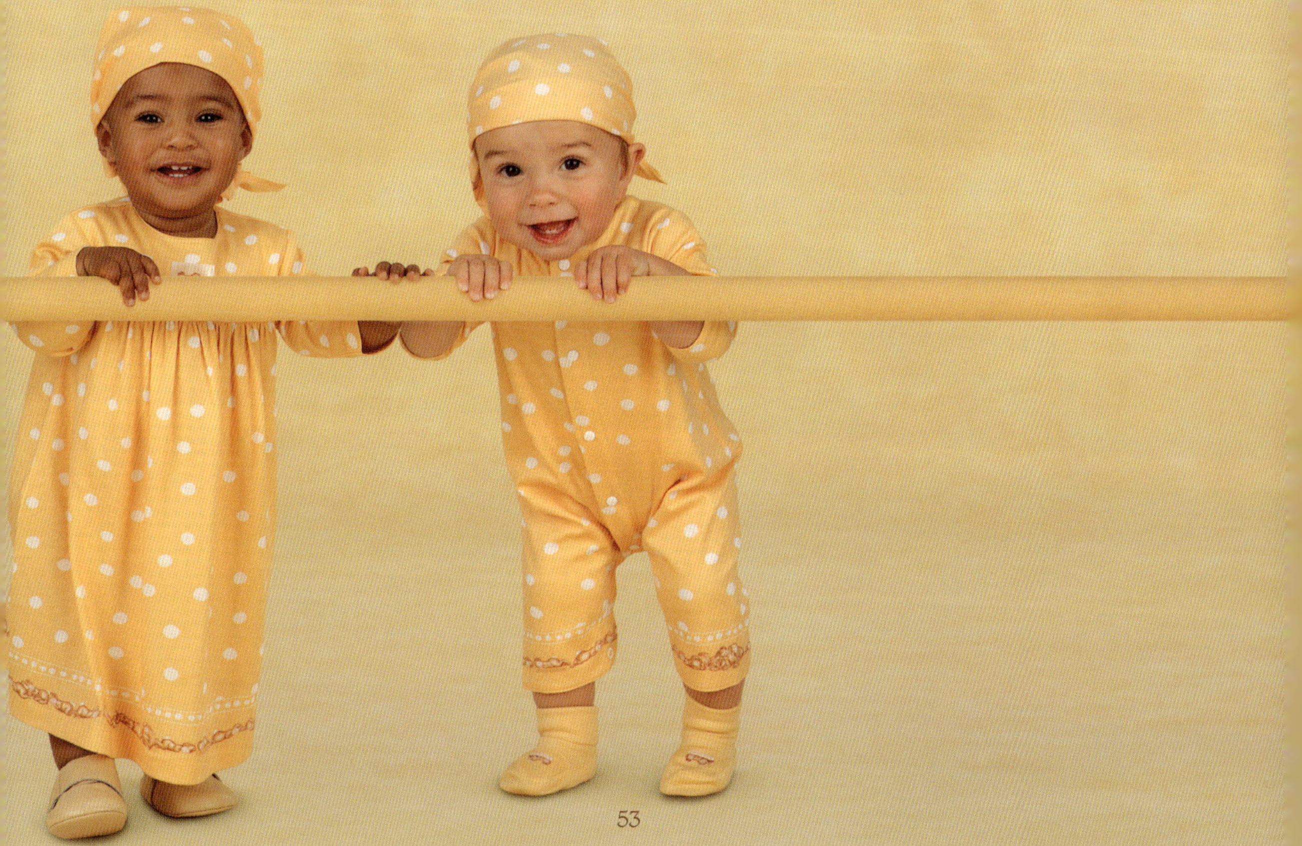

PRE-SCHOOL

I started on ______________________

My pre-school is called ______________________

____

My friends there are ______________________

____

____

____

____

____

____

____

What I like to do there

Comments

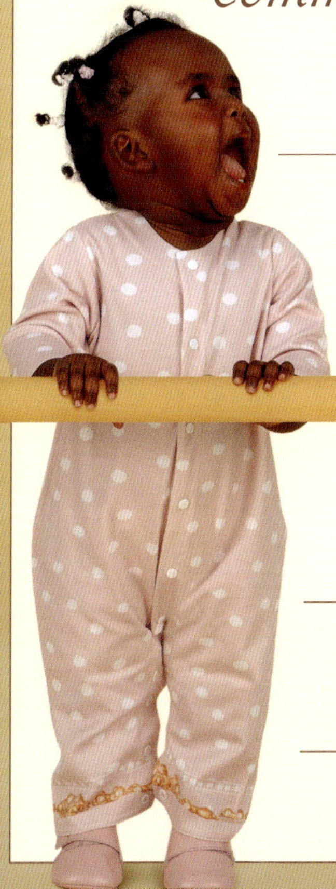

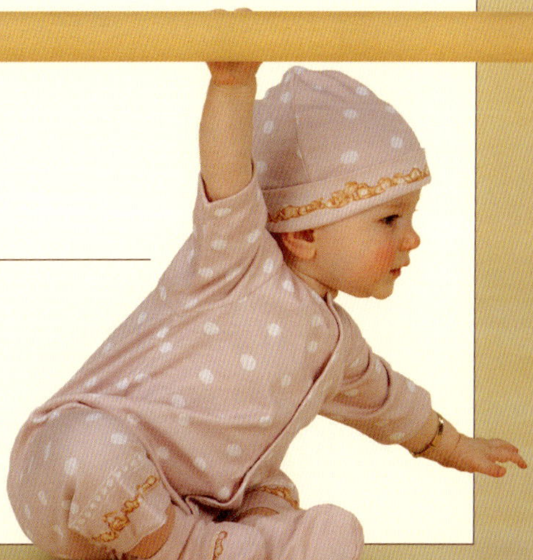

MY FIFTH BIRTHDAY

I live at ____________________

My height is ____________________

My weight is ____________________

Sayings ____________________

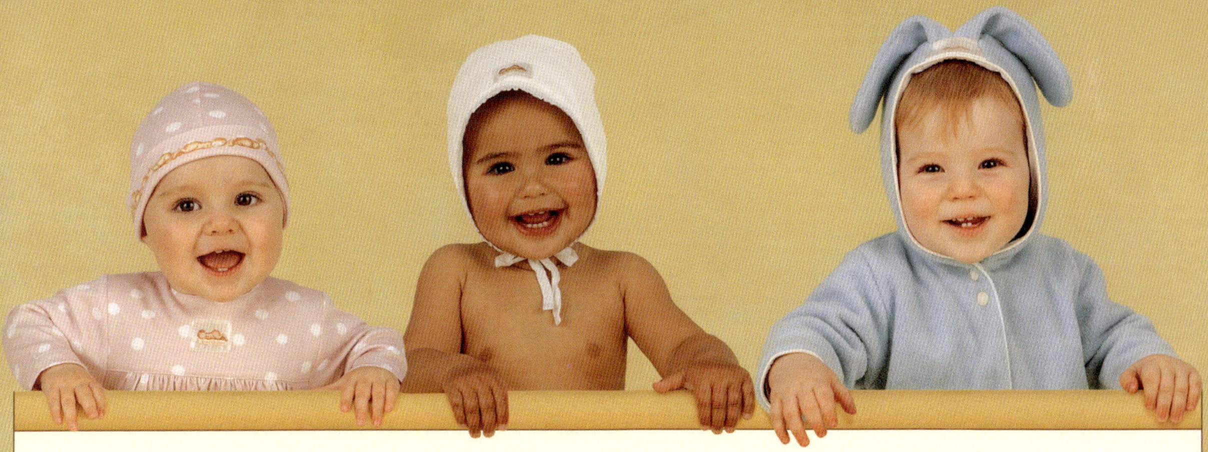

Toys

Pets

Books

MY PARTY

Date ______________________________

Place ______________________________

Friends & relatives there ______________________________

____

Presents ______________________________

____

____

____

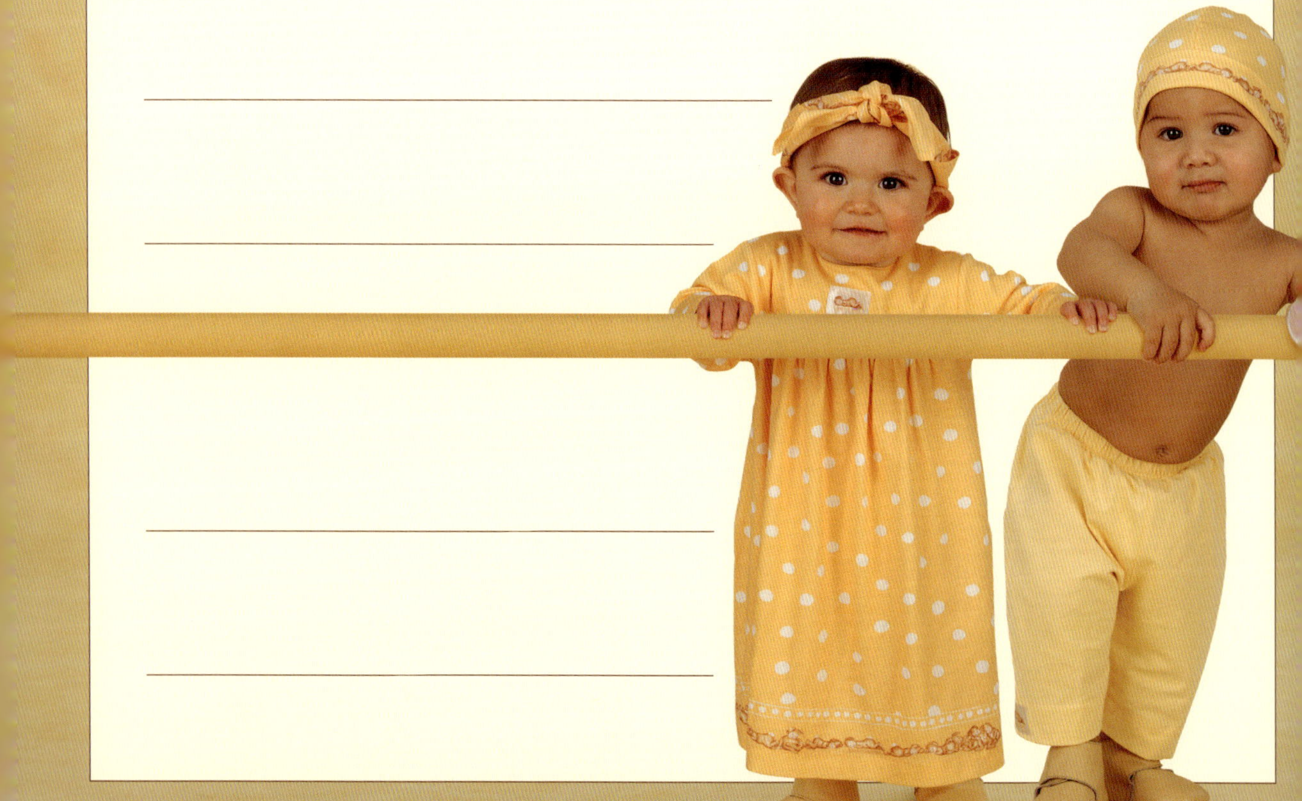

____

____

PHOTOGRAPHS

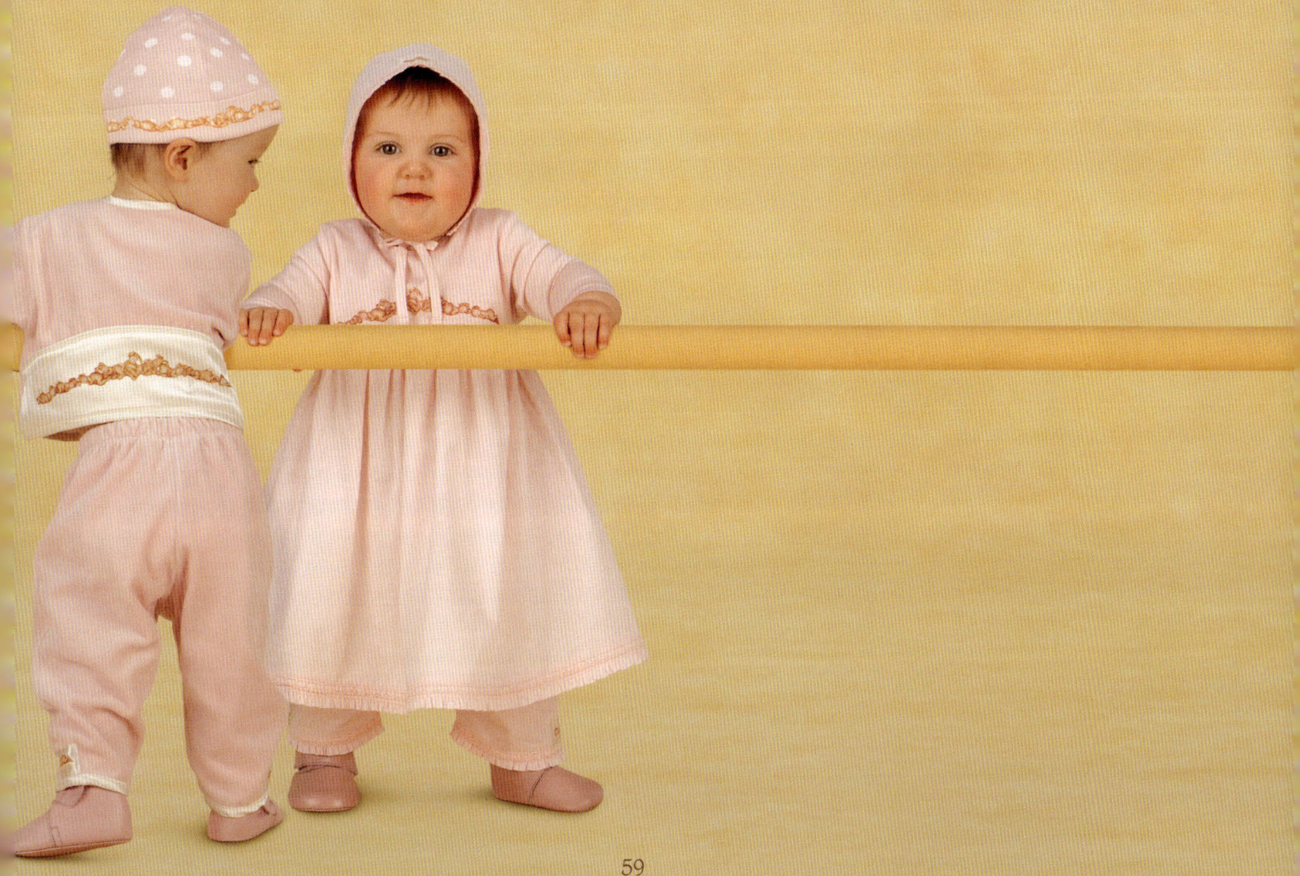

KINDERGARTEN

My first day at kindergarten was on ___________________

____

The name of my school is ______________________

____

My teacher is ___________________________

What I did on my first day ____________________

____

____

____

____

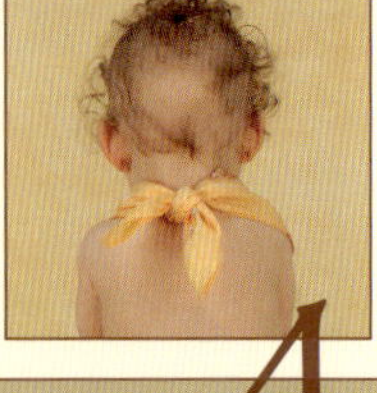

A

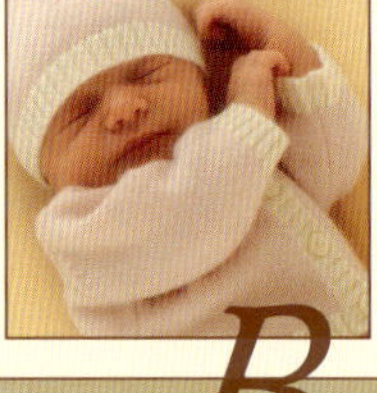

B

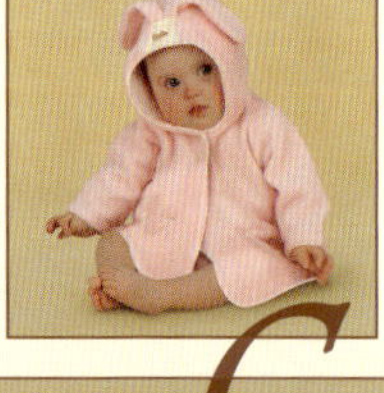

C

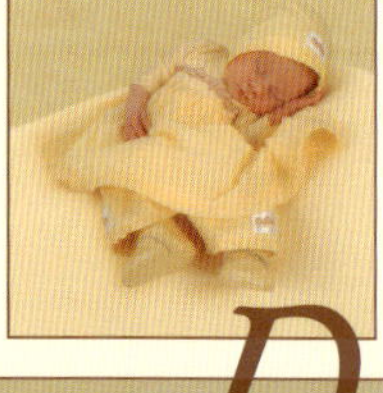

D

My friends are ______________________

____

____

____

Comments ______________________

____

____

____

____

E

F

G

H

DRAWINGS

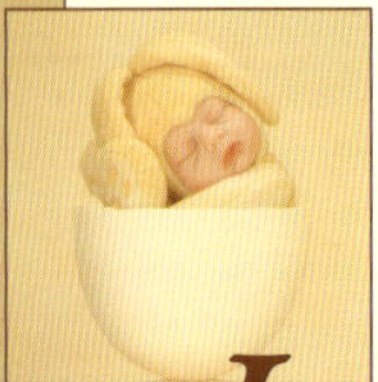

I

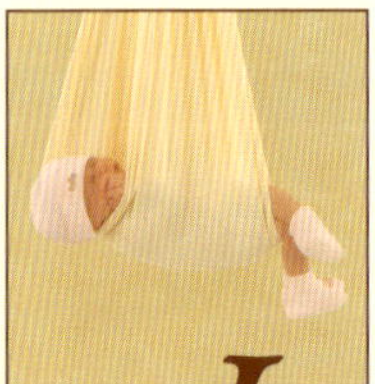

J

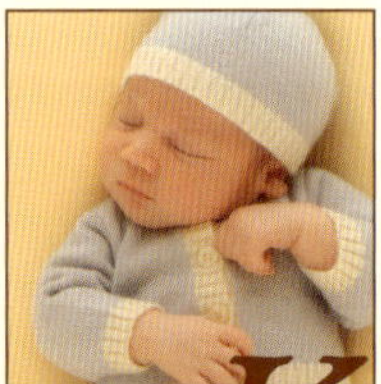

K

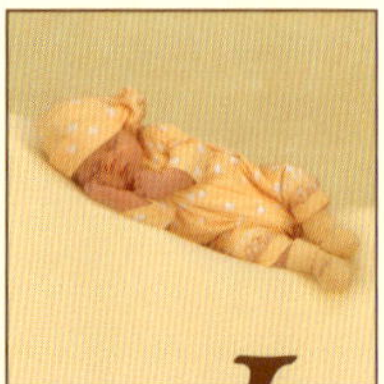

L

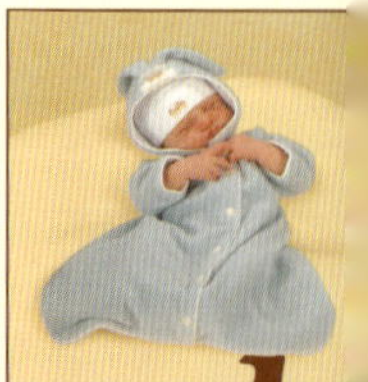

M

DRAWINGS

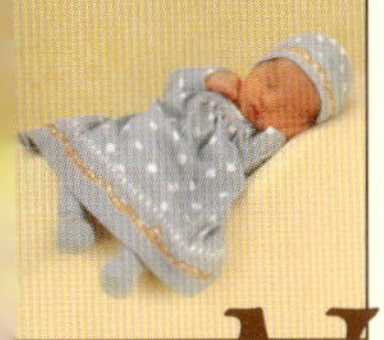
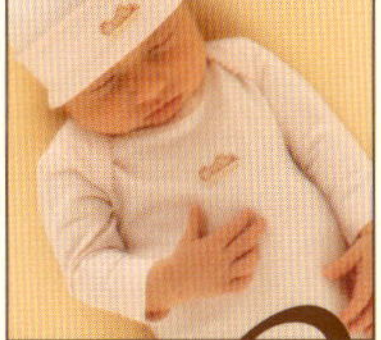
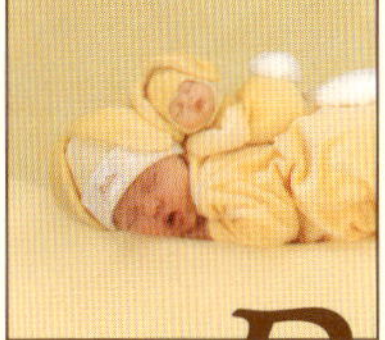
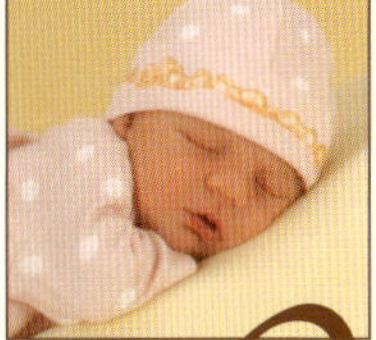
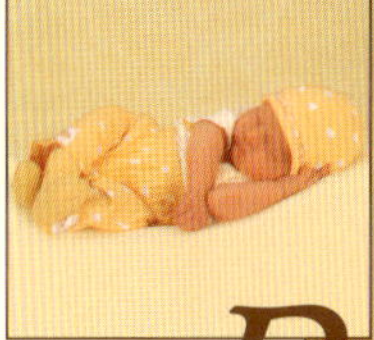

N O P Q R

WRITING

I could recite the alphabet ______________________

____

I started to write ______________________

I began to read ______________________

My writing ______________________

____

____

____

____

____

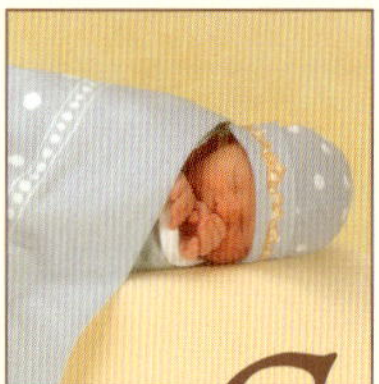

S

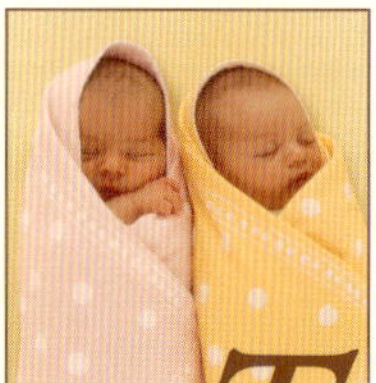

T

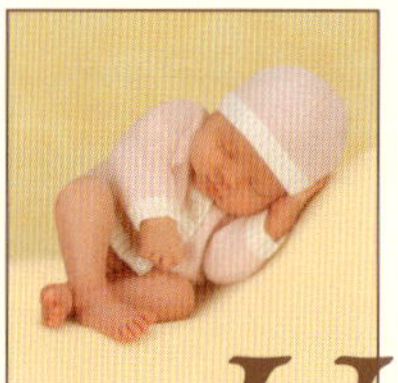

U

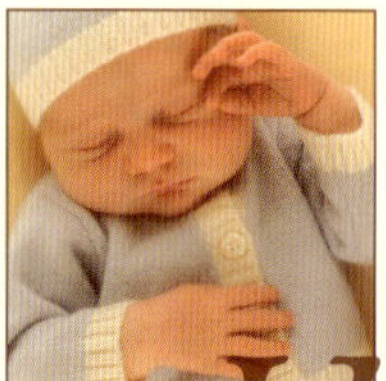

V

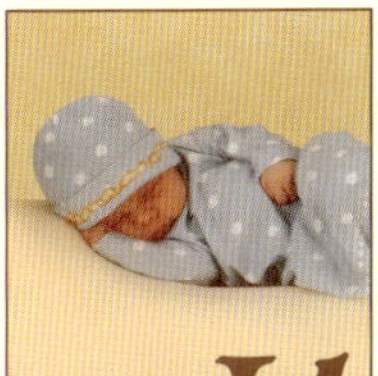

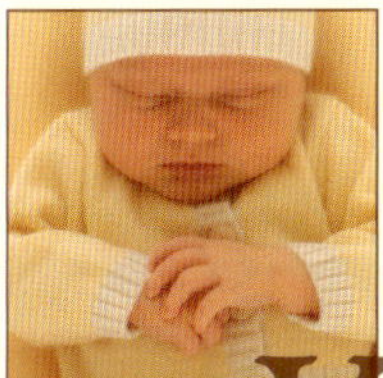

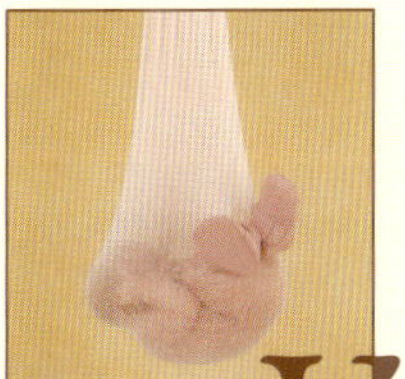

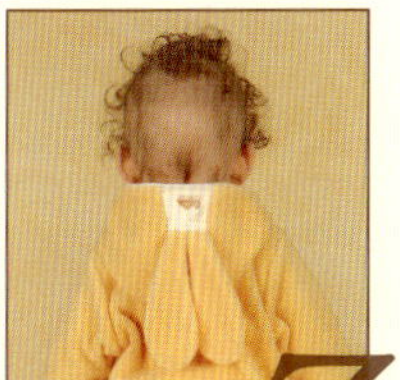

W X Y Z

Immunization

Age	Vaccine	Date given

Allergies

Illnesses

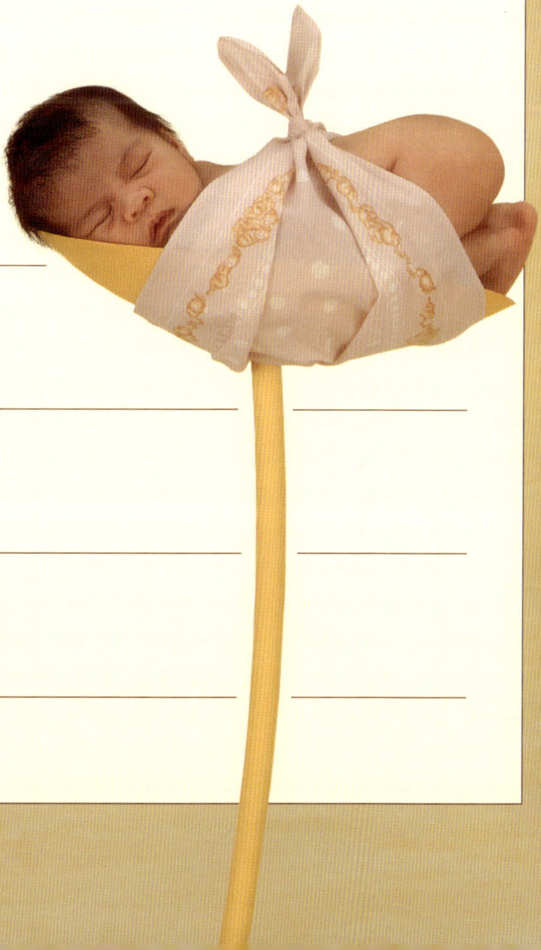

Comments

MY HEIGHT

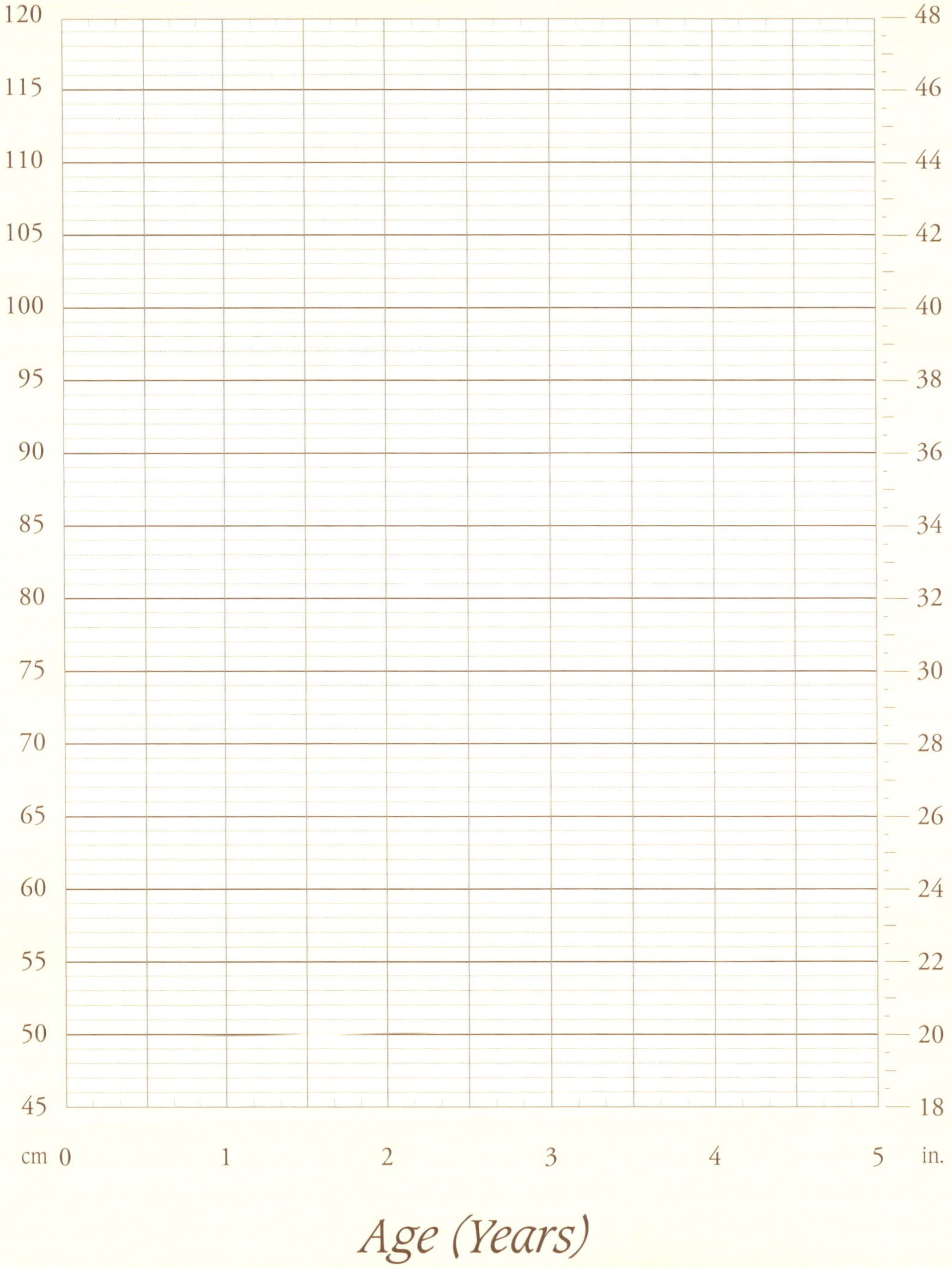
120
115
110
105
100
95
90
85
80
75
70
65
60
55
50
45
48
46
44
42
40
38
36
34
32
30
28
26
24
22
20
18
cm 0
1
2
3
4
5
in.
Age (Years)

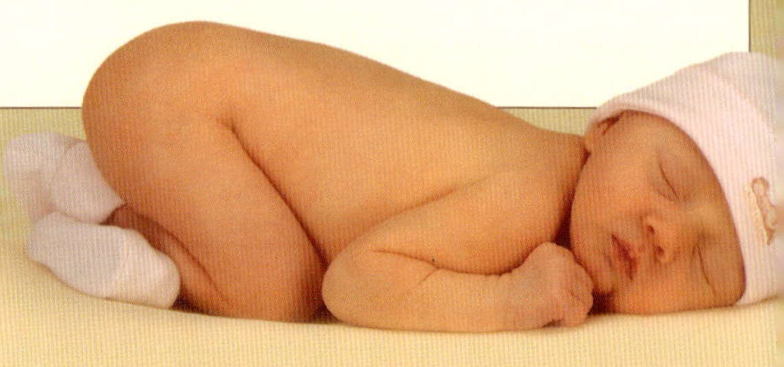

MY WEIGHT

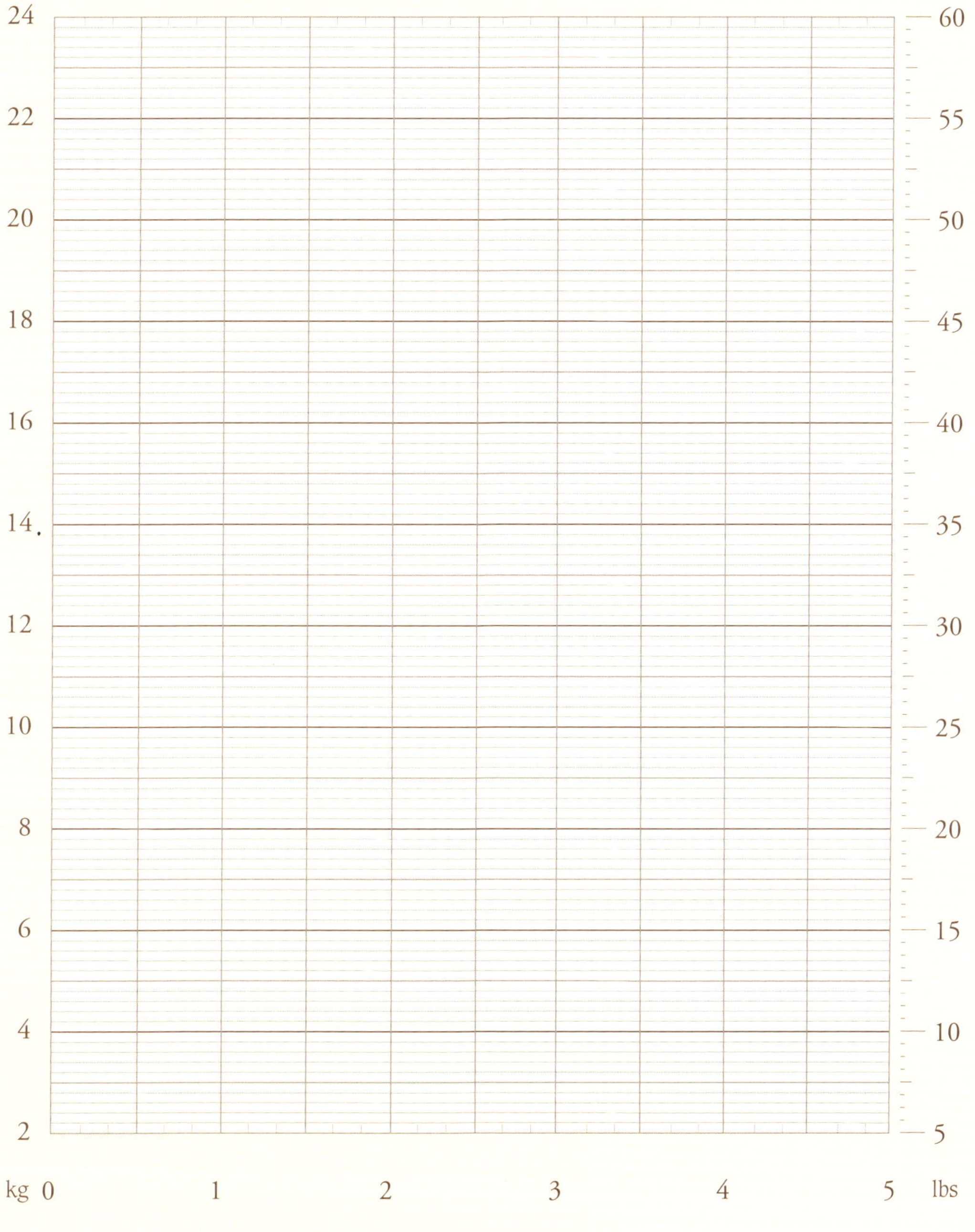
24
22
20
18
16
14
12
10
8
6
4
2
kg
0
1
2
3
4
5
lbs
60
55
50
45
40
35
30
25
20
15
10
5
Age (Years)

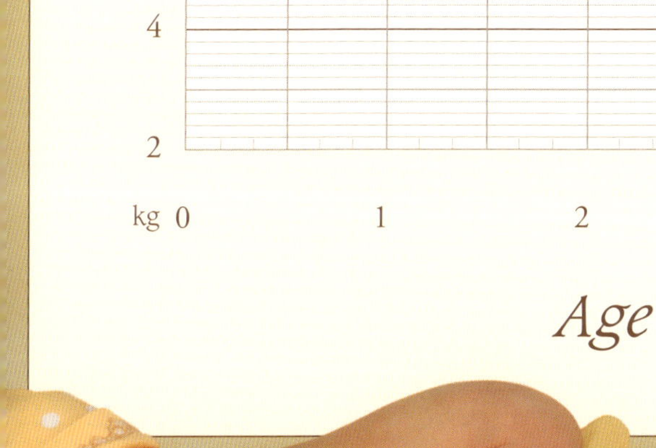

MY TEETH

Upper Jaw Dates

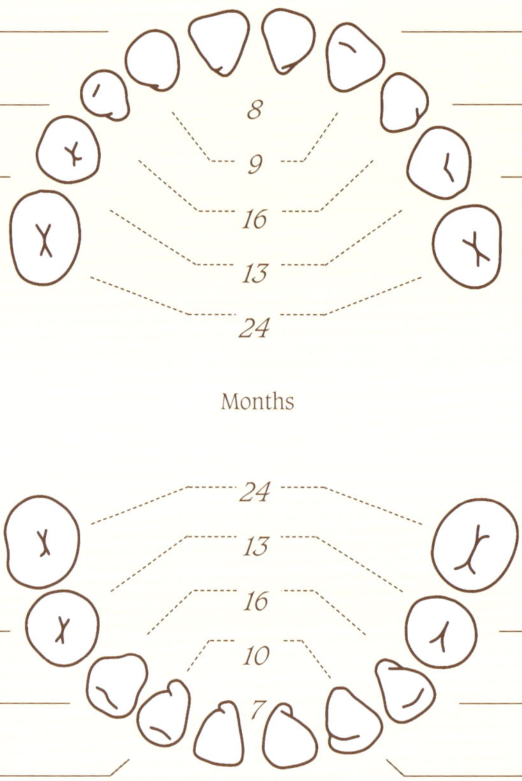

Lower Jaw Dates

Visits to the dentist

THE TOOTH FAIRY'S PAGE

I lost my first tooth ______________________________

My second tooth ______________________________

The Tooth Fairy left me ______________________________

____

Comments ______________________________

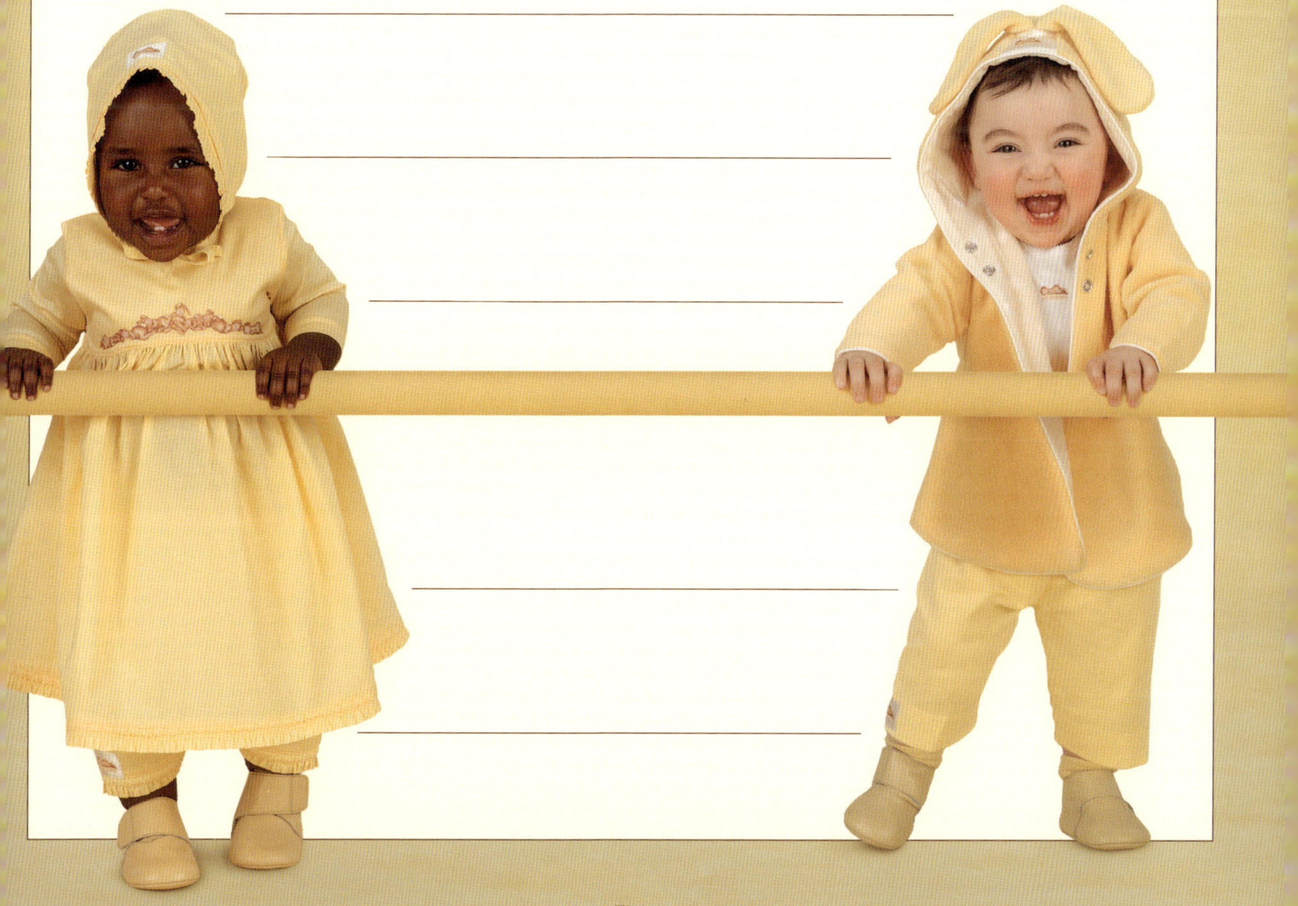

MY HANDPRINTS

At birth

At five years

MY FOOTPRINTS

At birth

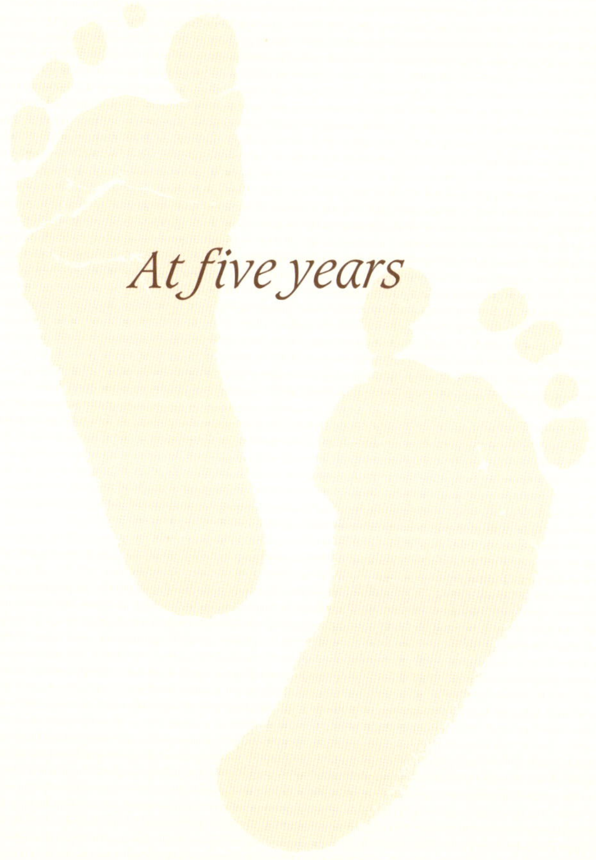

At five years

BIRTH STONES

JANUARY	. . .	Garnet - constancy, truth
FEBRUARY	. . .	Amethyst - sincerity, humility
MARCH	. . .	Aquamarine - courage, energy
APRIL	. . .	Diamond - innocence, success
MAY	. . .	Emerald - tranquillity
JUNE	. . .	Pearl - preciousness, purity
JULY	. . .	Ruby - freedom from care, chastity
AUGUST	. . .	Moonstone - joy
SEPTEMBER	. . .	Sapphire - hope, chastity
OCTOBER	. . .	Opal - reflecting every mood
NOVEMBER	. . .	Topaz - fidelity, loyalty
DECEMBER	. . .	Turquoise - love, success

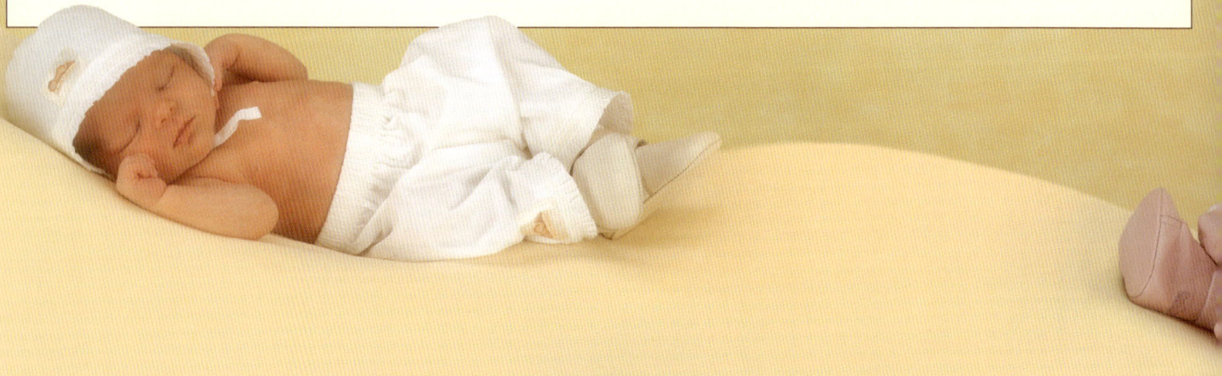

FLOWERS

JANUARY	. . .	Snowdrop - pure and gentle
FEBRUARY	. . .	Carnation - bold and brave
MARCH	. . .	Violet - modest
APRIL	. . .	Lily - virtuous
MAY	. . .	Hawthorn - bright and hopeful
JUNE	. . .	Rose - beautiful
JULY	. . .	Daisy - wide-eyed and innocent
AUGUST	. . .	Poppy - peaceful
SEPTEMBER	. . .	Morning Glory - easily contented
OCTOBER	. . .	Cosmos - ambitious
NOVEMBER	. . .	Chrysanthemum - sassy and cheerful
DECEMBER	. . .	Holly - full of foresight

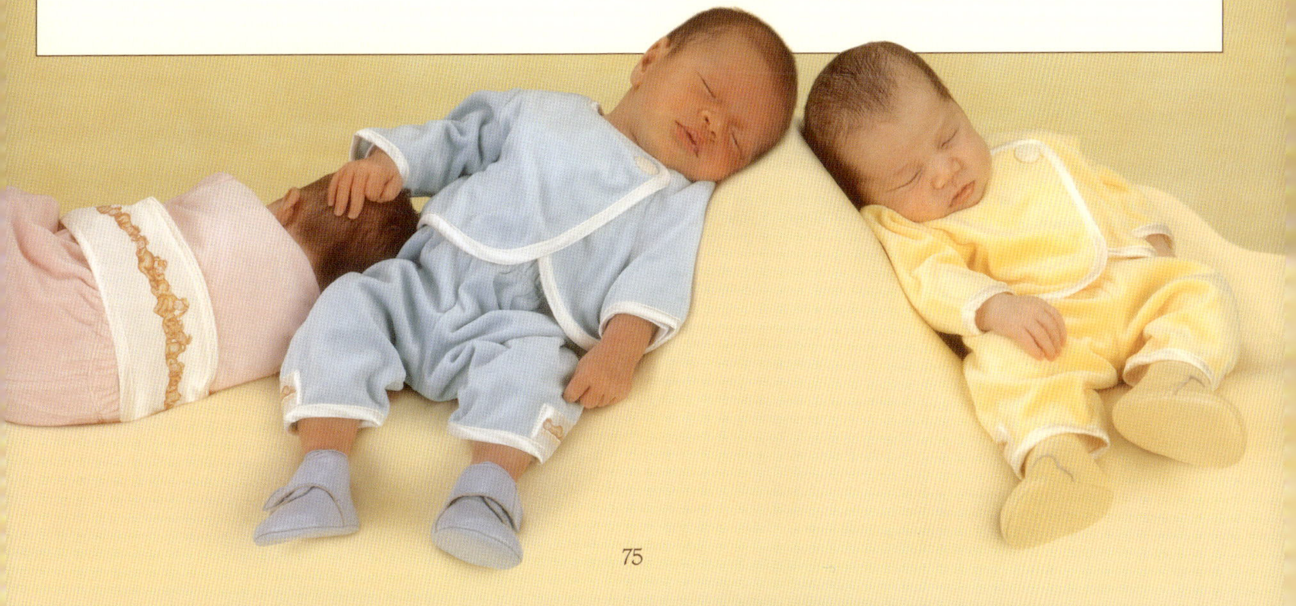

STAR SIGNS

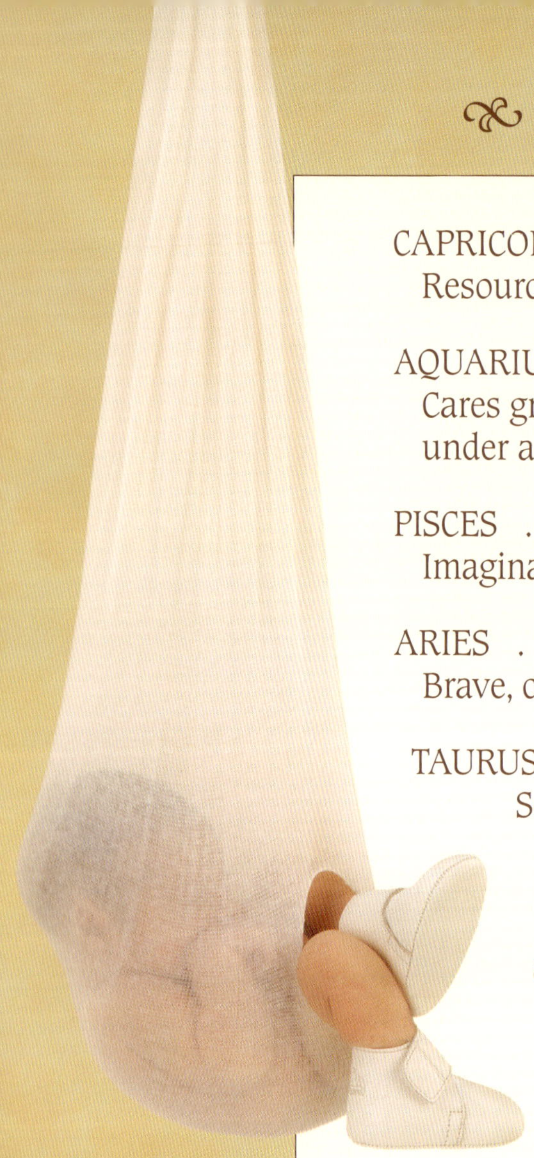

CAPRICORN . . . 22 December – 20 January
Resourceful, self-sufficient and responsible

AQUARIUS . . . 21 January – 18 February
Cares greatly for others, very emotional under a cool exterior

PISCES . . . 19 February – 19 March
Imaginative, sympathetic and tolerant

ARIES . . . 20 March – 20 April
Brave, courageous, energetic, loyal

TAURUS . . . 21 April – 21 May
Sensible, loves peace and stability

GEMINI . . . 22 May – 21 June
Unpredictable, lively, charming and witty

CANCER . . . 22 June – 22 July
Loves security and comfort

LEO . . . 23 July – 23 August
Idealistic, romantic, honorable and loyal

VIRGO . . . 24 August – 23 September
Shy, sensitive, and values knowledge

LIBRA . . . 24 September – 23 October
Diplomatic, full of charm and style

SCORPIO . . . 24 October – 22 November
Compassionate, proud and determined

SAGITTARIUS . . . 23 November – 21 December
Bold, impulsive, seeks adventure

CHINESE HOROSCOPES

RAT . . . 1936 . 1948 . 1960 . 1972 . 1984 . 1996 . 2008 . 2020 .
Humorous, honest, meticulous and hardworking

OX . . . 1937 . 1949 . 1961 . 1973 . 1985 . 1997 . 2009 . 2021 .
Intelligent, self confident, patient and trustworthy

TIGER . . . 1938 . 1950 . 1962 . 1974 . 1986 . 1998 . 2010 . 2022 .
Courageous, a natural leader, passionate and independent

RABBIT . . . 1939 . 1951 . 1963 . 1975 . 1987 . 1999 . 2011 . 2023 .
Peace loving, polite and intelligent, with artistic tendencies

DRAGON . . . 1940 . 1952 . 1964 . 1976 . 1988 . 2000 . 2012 . 2024 .
Intuitive, artistic, lucky and successful

SNAKE . . . 1941 . 1953 . 1965 . 1977 . 1989 . 2001 . 2013 . 2025 .
Philosophical, wise, calm and elegant

HORSE . . . 1930 . 1942 . 1954 . 1966 . 1978 . 1990 . 2002 . 2014 .
Cheerful, popular, independent. An adventurer at heart

RAM . . . 1931 . 1943 . 1955 . 1967 . 1979 . 1991 . 2003 . 2015 .
Good natured and generous with a good mind for business

MONKEY . . . 1932 . 1944 . 1956 . 1968 . 1980 . 1992 . 2004 . 2016 .
Witty, inventive, a fast learner with an excellent memory

ROOSTER . . . 1933 . 1945 . 1957 . 1969 . 1981 . 1993 . 2005 . 2017 .
Hardworking, social and confident. Family oriented

DOG . . . 1934 . 1946 . 1958 . 1970 . 1982 . 1994 . 2006 . 2018 .
Honest, faithful, responsible and prosperous

BOAR . . . 1935 . 1947 . 1959 . 1971 . 1983 . 1995 . 2007 . 2019 .
Sensitive, cultured, diligent. A perfect friend

PHOTOGRAPHS

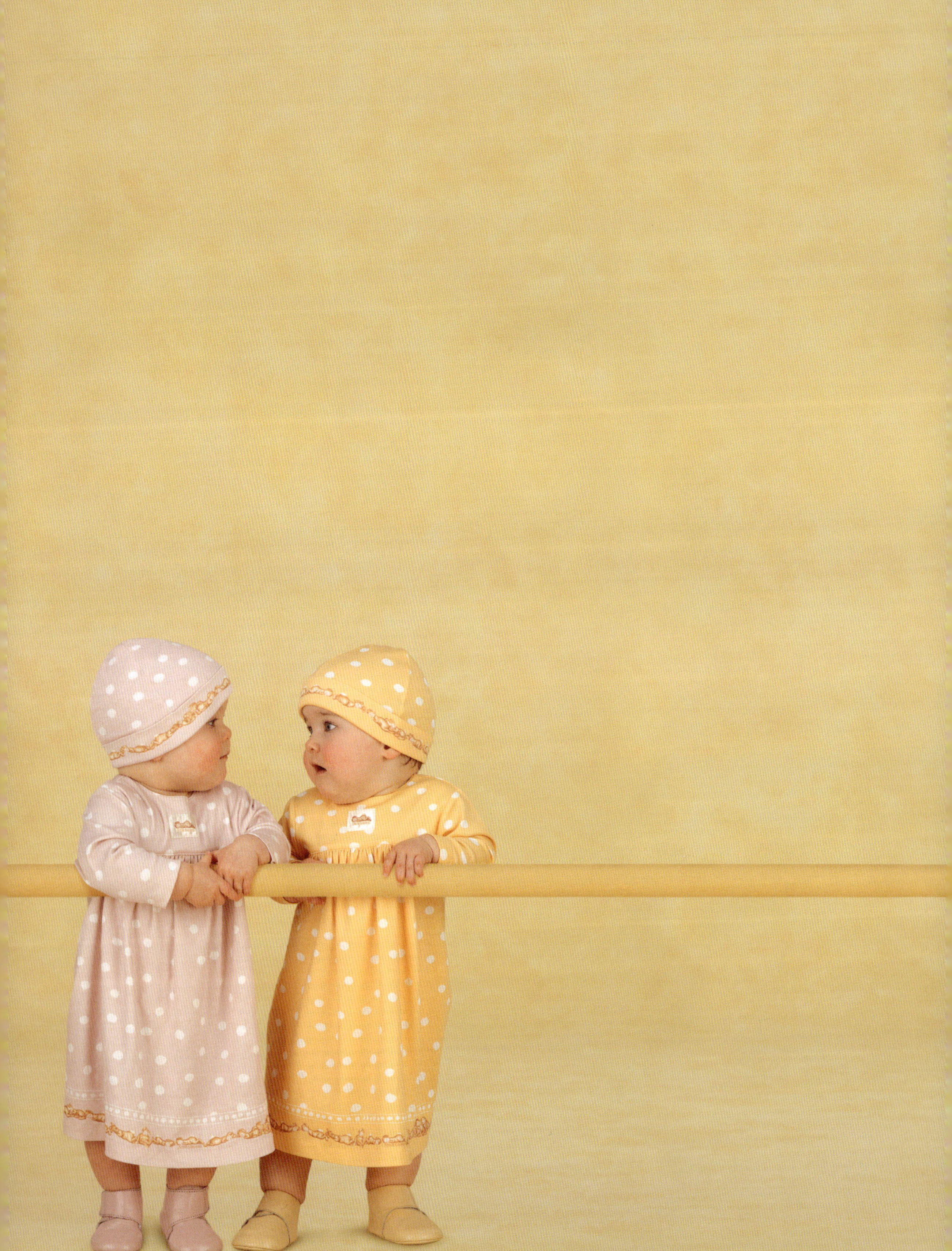

NOTES

Anne Geddes®

www.annegeddes.com

First published in 2003 by Photogenique Publishers
(a division of Hodder Moa Beckett)
4 Whetu Place, Mairangi Bay
Auckland, New Zealand

This edition published in North America in 2003
by Andrews McMeel Publishing
4520 Main Street, Kansas City, MO 64111-7701

Produced by Kel Geddes
Printed in China by Midas Printing Limited, Hong Kong

ISBN 0-7407-3414-8

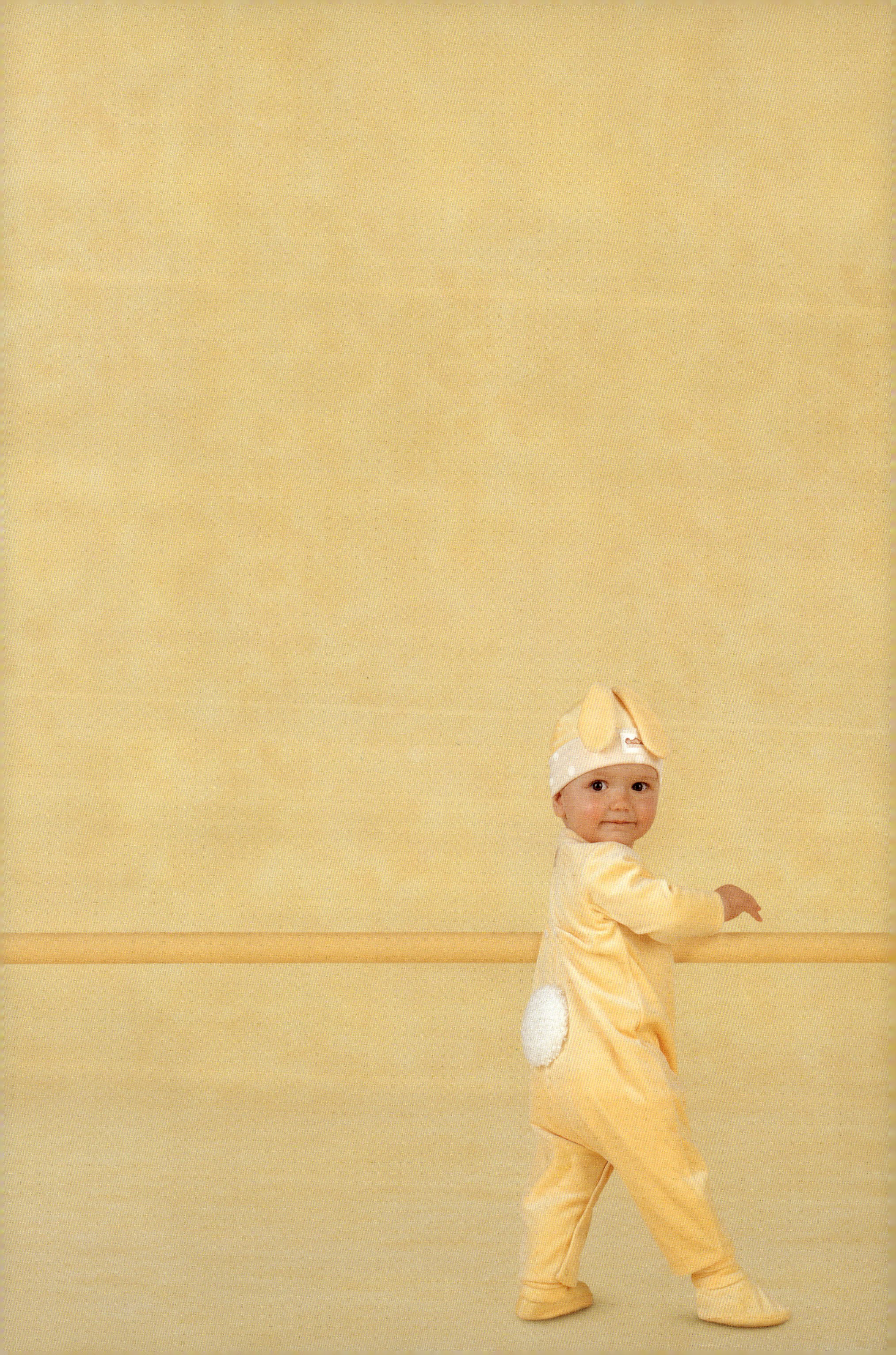

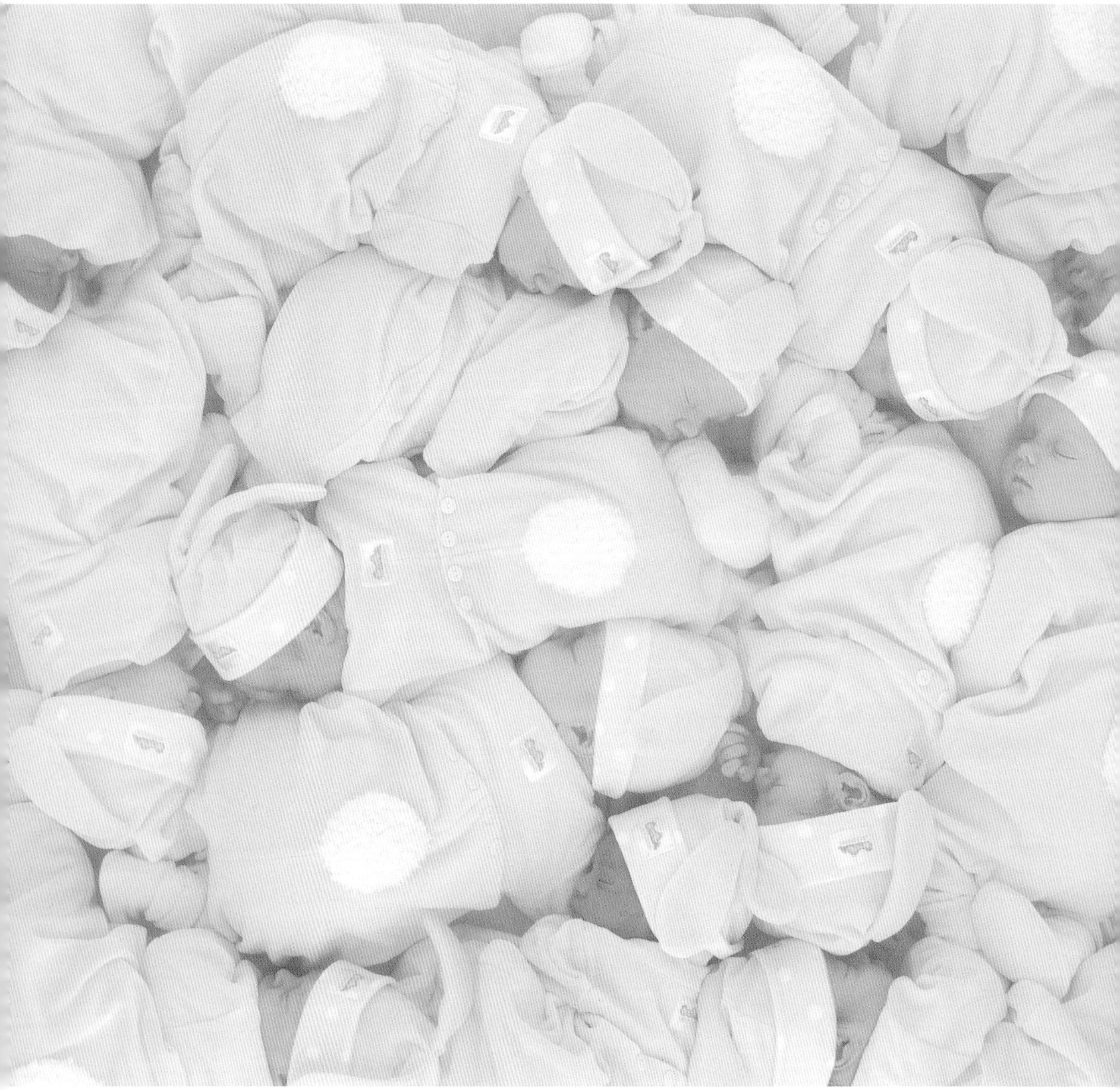